Papers of the Fifty-Fifth Algonquian Conference

Actes du cinquante-cinquième Congrès des Algonquinistes

PAPERS OF THE ALGONQUIAN CONFERENCES

ACTES DU CONGRÈS DES ALGONQUINISTES

Papers of the Fifty-Fifth Algonquian Conference

Actes du cinquante-cinquième Congrès des Algonquinistes

EDITED BY Inge Genee, Monica Macaulay, and Natalie Weber

MICHIGAN STATE UNIVERSITY PRESS | EAST LANSING

Michigan State University Press
East Lansing, Michigan 48823-5245

Library of Congress Cataloging-in-Publication Data
Names: Algonquian Conference (55th : 2023 : University of Alberta) | Genee, Inge, editor. | Macaulay, Monica Ann, editor. | Weber, Natalie, editor.
Title: Papers of the fifty-fifth Algonquian Conference = Actes du cinquante-cinquième Congrès des Algonquinistes / Inge Genee, Monica Macaulay, and Natalie Weber, Editors.
Other titles: Actes du cinquante-cinquième Congrès des Algonquinistes
Description: East Lansing, Michigan : Michigan State University Press, [2026] | Includes bibliographical references.
Identifiers: LCCN 2025024111 | ISBN 9781611865622 (paperback) | ISBN 9781609178086
Subjects: LCSH: Algonquian Indians—Congresses. | Algonquian languages—Congresses. | LCGFT: Conference papers and proceedings.
Classification: LCC E99.A35 A45 2023
LC record available at https://lccn.loc.gov/2025024111

Cover design by Erin Kirk
Cover detail of a quill box is used courtesy of Julie L. Loehr

Visit Michigan State University Press at *www.msupress.org*

Contents

Preface

Antti Arppe

The Fifty-fifth Algonquian Conference was held at the North Campus of the University of Alberta, in Edmonton, Alberta, from October 19 to 22, 2023. While located in Edmonton, we had significant support in the organization of this conference from our colleagues in other institutions on the Northern Western Plains, in particular Inge Genee at the University of Lethbridge.

If our prior counts are correct, this was the second time that this conference took place on the vast plains west of Manitoba and east of the Rocky Mountains, where many Algonquian peoples such as the nêhiyawak (Cree), Siksikaitsitapi (Blackfoot), Anishinaabeg (Ojibwe/Saulteaux/Anishinaabe), and the Métis, as well as other Indigenous peoples, continue to live. Consequently, like a dear child, Edmonton has many names in the local Algonquian tongues, known as *amiskwa-ci-wâskahikan* / ᐊᒥᐢᑲᐧᒌᐚᐢᑲᐦᐃᑲᐣ (Beaver Hills Lodge) by the Cree, *Omahkoyis* (Big Lodge) by the Blackfoot, and *Fort-des-Prairies* by the coureurs-des-bois. Like the previous time, we fretted in advance over what sort of impression the local weather would give the participants, of whom we had close to sixty, present either in-person or virtually. But again, we were treated to a quick succession of seasons, with almost summer-like warmth and sunshine on the evening of the welcome reception, which cooled off to regular fall temperatures over the next three days of the conference, capped with the first snows of the winter arriving only the day after.

To mark this second time in Edmonton, in the Canadian province of Alberta, we wanted to recognize the persistent Indigenous and Algonquian nature of this province. Alberta is the home for altogether 48 First Nations, having around 100,000 registered members, of whom 47% live on and 53% off reserve; Edmonton alone has 32,000 First Nations members. Crucially from an Algonquian perspective, 32 (67%) of these aforementioned 48 First Nations are predominantly Cree communities, and three (6%) Blackfoot communities. Therefore, we invited Indigenous keynote talks from three individuals/teams from Algonquian communities in Alberta, and were pleased to hear from Lisa Crowshoe (superintendent, Piikani Board of Education), Carla Badger, Rose Makinaw, Ida Bull, and Jolene Rain (Maskwacîs Curriculum Department, Maskwacîs Education Schools Commission), and Wayne Jackson (nêhiyawêwin Program Lead, University nuhelot'įne thaiyots'į nistameyimâkanak Blue Quills). This also marked the first time, to our knowledge, that the conference notice and call for papers were also posted in *nêhiyawêwin* (Plains Cree), one of the local languages that are a topic of the conference, in addition to the traditional English and French. In addition, we would like to note that the business meeting at this conference saw the establishment of an ad hoc committee for potentially founding at last a more formal Algonquian Association, the need for which has been discussed during many preceding conferences.

This fifty-fifth edition would not have been possible without the help and goodwill of many individuals and organizations. We were grateful to the immediately preceding organizers, Monica Macaulay, Marie-Odile Junker, and Andy Cowell, who shared (again) their experiences with us, greatly facilitating our own planning. We also want to recognize the significant efforts and initiative of our project coordinator, Héloïse Torck, whose management of our finances, registration, and reservations of conference locations, supervision of our volunteers, and attention that refreshments were ordered in advance in sufficient quantity relieved me of much anxiety. Similarly, our three local graduate student / postdoc organizers, Daniel Dacanay, Cameron Duval, and Katherine Schmirler, worked to make sure that the necessary conference preparations were realized in good order. Likewise, we are grateful to the local current or former student volunteers, in particular Lisa Andre, Athena Arlinghaus, Anna Cey, Lex Giesbrecht, Gabriella Gonzalez, Megan Harris, Padgett Hiew, Mary McCarthy, Devin Moore, and Alexander Rice, who ensured, for instance, that the classroom technology worked without a hitch, presentations kept to schedule, the out-of-town participants found their way to the welcome reception and the conference dinner, and coffee and tea remained plentiful, among many other small but important things. Also, we very much enjoyed the conference spaces that were made available for us at the UofA's modern Telus Centre, and we appreciated that the Alberta Gallery of Arts was able and willing to host us for the conference dinner, during which everyone got to enjoy the not-so-surprise entertainment that Bernie Francis graciously provided. Finally, we want to thank the Department of Linguistics (University of Alberta), the Kule Institute for Advanced Study (KIAS) for their Research Cluster Grant, and the Social Sciences and Humanities Research Council of Canada (SSHRC) for the generous funding that they provided to make possible the organization of this conference in Edmonton.

Additional Conference Papers

In addition to the papers published in this volume, the following papers were presented at the conference:

Jérémie Ambroise (Institut Tshakapesh and Carleton University, Uashat mak Mani-utenam (Innu)): What Do Chocolate and Dogs Have in Common in Innu?

Antti Arppe (University of Alberta), Atticus Harrigan (University of Alberta), Katherine Schmirler (University of Lethbridge), and Arok Wolvengrey (First Nations University of Canada): A Computational Model of Plains Cree Inflectional Morphology.

Julie Brittain (Memorial University), Ryan E. Henke (University of Wisconsin–Madison), and Shanley Allen (Technical University of Kaiserslautern): Preferred Argument Structure in Northern East Cree Child and Child-Directed Speech.

Chantale Cenerini (University of Saskatchewan) and Andrew Witzel: What's in a Code? Discussion and Pseudocode for Building Michif Verbs! Online Resource.

John-Paul Chalykoff (Michipicoten First Nation; Algoma University / Shingwauk Kinoomaage Gamig): Potential and Challenges in Adapting Anishinaabemowin to the Bescherelle Model.

David J. Costa (Myaamia Center at Miami University): Noun Gender in Miami-Illinois.

Andrew Cowell (University of Colorado, Boulder): An Initial Analysis of Story Sequences of Arapaho.

Kristy Eagle Bear (Iniskim/University of Lethbridge, Kainai Nation) and Inge Genee (University of Lethbridge): Blackfoot Views of the Blackfoot Language.

Sonja Fougère (University of British Columbia): Animacy as a Semantic Restriction.

Ken Fox (University of Lethbridge): Blackfoot Workshop.

Peter Grishin (MIT): Passamaquoddy-Wolastoqey Modals.

Peter Grishin (MIT) and Will Oxford (University of Manitoba): When Central Suffixes Agree with Peripheral Participants.

Corinne Kasper (University of Chicago, Pokagon Band of Potawatomi Indians): LDA in L2 Potawatomi.

Craig Kopris (Wyandot Nation): An Introduction to the Omisun Program in Virginia.

Hunter Lockwood (Myaamia Center at Miami University): Notes on Measurement and Mathematics in Miami-Illinois.

Hunter Lockwood (Myaamia Center at Miami University), Monica Macaulay (University of Wisconsin–Madison), and Vivian Nash (University of Wisconsin–Madison): Relative Roots: Form and Function.

Angela Mesic (University of Wisconsin–Milwaukee), Tessa Culleton (University of Wisconsin–Milwaukee), and Nathon Breu (University of Wisconsin–Milwaukee): Gidozhibii'amawaanaanig Gidoshkigiminaanig—The Importance of Phonemic Awareness in Ojibwemowin to Support Early Literacy.

Mary Nevins (Middlebury College): With as Much Faith as Many Equally Absurd Doctrines Are Observed in Christendom.

Mykelle Pacquing (Toronto Metropolitan University and York University): The Use of Natural Language Processing, Artificial Intelligence, and Social Robotics for Anishinaabemowin Revitalization and Reclamation.

Richard A. Rhodes (University of California, Berkeley) and Wayne Leman (SIL International and Chief Dull Knife College; Ninilchik Traditional Council): On the Historical Relationship between Cheyenne and Arapahoan.

Fatiha Sadat and Antoine Cadotte (Université de Quebec à Montréal): First Results of Collaboration with Innu-aimun Translators to Initiate the Development of Translation Assistance Tools.

Heather Souter (Prairies to Woodlands Indigenous Language Revitalization Circle / University of Winnipeg), Verna DeMontigny (Prairies to Woodlands Indigenous Language Revitalization Circle), Olivia N. Sammons (Prairies to Woodlands Indigenous Language Revitalization Circle / First Nations University of Canada), David Huggins-Daines (Prairies to Woodlands Indigenous Language Revitalization Circle), Carmen Leeming (Prairies to Woodlands Indigenous Language Revitalization Circle), Marlee Patterson (Prairies to Woodlands Indigenous Language Revitalization Circle), Talula Schegel (Prairies to Woodlands Indigenous Language Revitalization Circle), Kade Ferris (Prairies to Woodlands Indigenous Language Revitalization Circle), and Tiara Opissinow (Prairies to Woodlands Indigenous Language Revitalization Circle): Bridging Southern Michif Digital Resources with Language Revitalization.

Lucy Thomason (Smithsonian Institution): The Sky Was Even the Color of Flame: The Use of Color Terms in Michelson's Meskwaki Literature.

Shanti Ulfsbjorninn (Memorial University of Newfoundland): Initial Change in Sheshatshiu Innu-Aimûn: Infixation and Feature Packing.

Natalie Weber (Yale University): Blackfoot Words Database: Reflecting on our Methods and Projects.

misi-mîkiwâhp pêsêkinosa ohci

A Corpus of Miscellaneous Plains Cree Texts

Daniel Dacanay and Antti Arppe

Due to its wide geographic distribution and (relatively) large speaking population, Plains Cree (ISO:crk, endonymically known as *nêhiyawêwin*) has historically been comparatively well-documented from the perspective of a North American Indigenous language. Extensive dictionaries have existed since the mid-19th century (e.g., Lacombe 1874), with new dictionaries being written and updated to the present day (e.g., Wolvengrey 2011). Pedagogical tools, both self-guided (Bontogon et al. 2018) and curricular in nature (Alberta Education 2009), have been developed (although not universally adopted) in the language, as have extensive metalinguistic descriptions of the language (e.g., Wolfart 1973). Finally, digital tools for Plains Cree, although relatively new, are being developed in various forms (e.g., Harrigan et al. 2017; Harrigan et al. 2019; Poulin et al. 2023; Arppe et al. 2023a; Arppe et al. 2023b). Broadly speaking then, although still far behind that of Canada's two official languages, the level of existing lexicographic and grammatical documentation of Plains Cree compares favorably with those of most other North American Indigenous languages. This paper will therefore focus on the current state of one final element of Plains Cree documentation, that is, its extant text corpora, and will detail the development and contents of the Miscellaneous Cree Text corpus, a sizable new addition to the body of existing Cree corpus resources.

Plains Cree Writing Systems

To discuss textual corpora in Plains Cree, it is first necessary to outline written Plains Cree more generally. To begin, Plains Cree is, and always has been, a predominantly oral language. Although evidence for natively produced Cree writing is seen as early as the latter half of the 19th century (e.g., Bird et al. 1888), most Cree speakers seldom use the language in written form. Nonetheless, written Plains Cree exists in a state of digraphia, split between Cree syllabics and the Standard Roman Orthography. Syllabics, an abugida-like syllabary initially developed in the 1830s by Methodist missionary James Evans to transcribe Ojibwe, are dominant in texts written in the late 19th and early 20th centuries. Having spread organically to Cree communities with little formal teaching (Murdoch 1981), spelling conventions in Plains Cree syllabics are highly decentralized and vary substantially between authors. Early romanization of Cree largely shares this lack of consistent orthographic rules, with early authors in both systems generally following their own idiosyncratic conventions. However, over the course of the 1970s and 1980s, collaboration between linguists such as Douglas Ellis (1973), David Pentland (1977), H. C. Wolfart (1973), and Freda Ahenakew (1987), aided by leading elders from across Alberta and Saskatchewan, led to the formation and adoption of a Standard Roman Orthography (or SRO) for Plains Cree. The SRO has since become the principal writing system in linguistic and pedagogical texts and is becoming increasingly widespread in general usage. However, as previously mentioned, most fluent Cree speakers are not fully literate in either system, and many authors still write using idiosyncratic romanizations, simply writing "what [they] hear" (Okimāsis and Wolvengrey 2008).

Plains Cree Corpora

Aside from the novel corpus discussed in this paper, there exist four major textual corpora of Plains Cree, totaling between them ~220,000 word tokens. This places the Plains Cree corpus size above that of most North American Indigenous languages — for example Choctaw (with ~50,000 tokens) (Brixey et al. 2018), Mi'kmaq (with ~76,000 tokens) (Maheshwari et al. 2018), or Cherokee (with ~206,000 tokens) (Zhang et al. 2020) — although still behind some more widely spoken Indigenous languages such as Nahuatl (with ~1.2 million tokens) (Gutierrez-Vasques et al. 2016) or Inuktitut (with ~8 million tokens) (Joanis et al. 2020), and vastly behind even minor corpora of majority languages such as English (e.g., ~500 million tokens in the descriptively titled Corpus of American Soap Operas (Davies 2011), or ~18 billion tokens in the broader News on the Web Corpus (Davies 2016)). In order of total size, the four major Plains Cree corpora are the Ahenakew-Wolfart Corpus, the Bloomfield Corpus, the EdTeKLA Corpus, and the Spoken Dictionary of Maskwacîs Cree, each of which is detailed below.

The largest extant corpus of Plains Cree is the Ahenakew-Wolfart Corpus (AW), a corpus consisting primarily of stories, personal reminiscences, and lectures collected from L1 Plains Cree speakers (all of whom were raised in either monolingually or primarily Plains Cree–speaking households, including several speakers who were monolinguals themselves) from across Alberta and Saskatchewan between 1982 and 1996 by Freda Ahenakew and H. C. Wolfart. This corpus totals 79,930 tokens of Plains Cree text, representing 18,212 types. For the purposes of this text, we define "tokens" as any space-separated character strings (with hyphenated polymorphemic words (such as *ta-mosci-wâpahtamihk* 'it is simply to be seen', being classed single tokens), and "types" as any unique tokens (albeit with some normalization of common orthographic variation: i.e., *ta-mosci-wâpahtamihk* (with a circumflex length marker) and *ta-mosci-wāpahtamihk* (with a macron length marker) are listed as constituting a single type, despite their orthographic distinctness). All of the tokens in this corpus have been written in the SRO, and more recently have been morphosyntactically tagged through a combination of computational means (see Arppe et al. 2020; Schmirler 2022) and human annotation.

The Bloomfield Corpus (BF) represents the second largest corpus in the collection at 72,475 tokens, representing 15,267 types. BF consists largely of personal reminiscences, anecdotes, and traditional legends, collected by Leonard Bloomfield from elders living on the Sweetgrass First Nation reserve in southern Saskatchewan throughout the 1920s and 1930s (Bloomfield 1930; 1934). Although initially written in Bloomfield's own orthography, the contents of these texts have more recently been converted into the SRO through the work of Kevin Russell and H. C. Wolfart, who also provided full morphological analyses throughout, in addition to analyses provided computationally (Schmirler 2022).

The EdTeKLA Corpus (ED) is a miscellaneous corpus consisting largely of hymnal lyrics, educational materials, and interviews, as well as other assorted text types, developed by the Educational Technology, Knowledge, Language, and Learning Analytics Research Group (EdTeKLA) at the University of Alberta (Teodorescu et al. 2022). Consisting of 49,038 tokens, representing 15,202 types, this corpus is distinct from AW and BF in that it was compiled for use in the development of natural language processing technologies, as opposed to being intended for linguistic analysis. Nonetheless, its contents are still parseable by linguists, being rendered in the SRO and morphologically tagged.

The final major Plains Cree lexical resource used is the Spoken Dictionary of Maskwacîs Cree (SD), a collection of 20,300 individual recorded words and phrases with accompanying audio provided by several dozen elders from Maskwacîs, a Cree settlement in Central Alberta (Arppe et al. 2023b; Poulin et al. 2023). We (that is, the first and second author) were heavily involved in the creation of SD, having constructed it at the request of the Maskwacîs Education Schools Commission with the express intention of using it for further language documentation and revitalization projects such as that described here. SD is not strictly a corpus, instead being more akin to a dictionary-like database of lexical entries; however, like the three aforementioned corpora, SD is rendered entirely in the SRO and has been fully morphologically tagged.

One consistent factor across these existing corpora and databases (with the exception of ED) is their use of original, purpose-collected texts (or, in the case of SD, purpose-elicited sentences). Rather than repurposing existing Cree writings to form a corpus of incidental materials (as is done for most large corpora for majority languages), AW, BF, and SD consist entirely of materials that were elicited, recorded, and compiled for the express purpose of creating a body of representative corpus literature. However, these texts are far from all of the writing that exists in Plains Cree. Rather, there is a wealth of existing written Cree material created with no overt intention of language documentation, being instead made, as the written word so often is, to serve the more mundane purposes of transmitting and disseminating information. These miscellaneous, pedestrian works of written Cree, publicly available but as yet unaccounted for in existing corpora, are to be the focus of the remainder of this paper; in particular, we will outline their contents, provenance, and the process by which we have compiled a substantial portion of these works into a new corpus of assorted written Plains Cree, henceforth known as the Miscellaneous Cree Texts corpus (MCT), with this resource being larger in token size than any Cree corpus preceding it.

Textual Composition

The MCT consists of 553 individual texts, divided into four subcorpora based on their origins. These are texts produced by organs of the federal or provincial government(s) of Canada (GC), miscellaneous texts produced by corporations, private individuals, or local authorities (MISC), texts produced by the Cree Literacy Network (CLN), and pedagogical texts (PED). The texts in all four of these subcorpora were found entirely through free, publicly available online repositories (see the AVAILABILITY section) and are all natively bilingual; that is, each individual text was either a Cree document with an accompanying English translation, or a Cree translation of an originally English document. Thus, each .txt file in the corpus contains the full Cree and English versions of the relevant text, matched and parallelized on the sentence level (see the FORMATTING section).

Governmental Texts (GC)

Since the late 2010s (and to a lesser extent beforehand), the federal government of Canada, the provincial governments of Alberta and Saskatchewan, and the government of the Northwest Territories have been intermittently publishing Plains Cree translations of various informational documents, governmental declarations, and speeches, all originally written in English. There is little consistency in the schedule by which new translations are created, nor any apparent pattern in which documents receive such translations; however, altogether, roughly two to three are published each month, with the federal government producing a substantial majority of these. These texts are generally written in some variation of the SRO, although their authors and translators are virtually never credited. In total, GC consists of 96 distinct texts, with these documents varying in length from 8 tokens to 17,102 tokens, with the mean token count being 2,021 (median 1,027). The total token count between all 96 texts (excluding punctuation) is 182,293 (79,327 Cree tokens and 102,966 English tokens), representing 20,925 Cree word types.

Although explicitly intended for public consumption, and therefore freely accessible online, the GC texts are highly decentralized in their storage. None of the relevant governmental websites have any consistent internal mark-up system to indicate which documents have Cree translations, nor any curated repositories containing exhaustive (or even extensive) lists of them. As such, the only reliable method that we have found to locate Cree language documents in the archives of these sites has been to use lists of high frequency Cree lexemes as site-wide search criteria. For example, to begin, we entered the most common item from existing Plains Cree word frequency lists, êkwa 'and, also; then' (Wolvengrey 2011), as well as its common orthographic variants ēkwa and *ekwa*, as a query on a site-wide search of the federal government's website (https://www.canada.ca) and manually reviewed all search results to extract any documents containing Plains Cree text. Then, we searched the second most frequent Plains Cree word, *ohci* 'from there; with; for' (Wolvengrey 2011), manually reviewed those results, and extracted any documents containing Plains Cree text that were not extracted in the initial search. We then repeated this process until no new Cree documents could be found (typically, using ten of the most common lexical items was sufficient), and then reapplied the process from the beginning on each relevant governmental or ministerial website. Although laborious, this process ultimately appears to have yielded a thorough overview of the Cree contents of each website searched.

Miscellaneous Texts (MISC)

In addition to Cree translations of English documents published by organs of the state, in recent years, a large number of private organizations have also begun issuing similar Plains Cree document translations of their own. Many of these are corporate entities, such as media outlets, banks, law firms, and educational institutions; however, a sizable portion are also nonprofit organizations, typically environmentalist groups, public health advocacy centers, art galleries, and political commentators. In addition to translated Cree documents from these sources, the MISC subcorpus also contains public Cree-language blog posts, Cree interview transcripts, and publicly available written Cree stories not represented in any other existing corpora. Similar to the GC texts, these documents were scattered dispersedly across publicly accessible Internet sources, with no centralized directory of any kind. As such, these texts were collected using the same high frequency search query method as was employed for the GC subcorpus, applied this time to a Google search. As might be expected from their miscellaneous nature, orthographic conventions varied substantially in these texts, with authors and translators sometimes, but not always, being credited (see section LIMITATIONS). In total, the MISC subcorpus consists of 223 individual texts with a total token count of 239,493 (96,267 Cree and 143,226 English), representing 31,442 Cree word types. Texts ranged in length from 24 tokens to 20,360 tokens, with a mean token count of 1,175 (median 406).

The Cree Literacy Network (CLN)

The Cree Literacy Network (CLN) is a language advocacy group, founded to promote daily Cree language usage, cultural literacy, and the Standard Roman Orthography. Through their website, https://creeliteracy.org, the CLN has been posting stories, poems, songs, educational materials, and blog-style updates on various language documentation projects at a regular interval of several posts per month since 2013. Unlike the GC and MISC subcorpora, CLN posts are not only centralized (through the https://creeliteracy.org website), but posts that contain Cree text are also explicitly marked in their titles. Other relevant metadata, such as the name and language background of the author, are provided for 97.3% (211/217) of posts containing language data. Given its status as an advocacy group for Cree literacy, CLN posts are also uniformly rendered in the SRO. In total, the CLN subcorpus contains 217 texts totaling 35,596 tokens (12,419 Cree tokens and 23,177 English tokens) and 5,946 Cree word types, with texts ranging in length from 7 tokens to 3,781 tokens, with a mean token count of 197 (median 79).

Pedagogical Texts (PED)

The final, and least voluminous, subcorpus is that of pedagogical texts (PED), being composed of running texts found as exercises or examples in educational works such as textbooks. These are typically either short stories, scripted dialogues, or loosely connected lists of phrase translations, typically constructed in an intentionally simplistic or formulaic fashion for ease of learner understanding. Being texts published chiefly by well-known Cree educators, these texts have ample information on the name(s) and language background(s) of the authors. As mentioned, this is

TABLE 1. Token and type counts for the various subcorpora of MCT

SUBCORPUS	TOKEN COUNT (CREE) (EXCLUDING PUNCTUATION)	CREE TYPE COUNT	CREE TEXT COUNT
GC	182,293 (79,327)	20,925	96
MISC	239,493 (96,267)	31,442	223
CLN	35,596 (12,419)	5,946	217
PED	15,991 (5,186)	2,693	17
Total	473,373 (193,199)	61,006	553

the smallest subcorpus, consisting of 17 texts totaling 15,991 tokens (5,186 Cree, 10,805 English) and 2,693 Cree word types, ranging in size from 197 tokens to 7,037 tokens, with a mean of 1,311 tokens (median 435).

Formatting

Each text included in the corpus was rendered as a UTF-8 encoded .txt file, containing the source URL of the text followed by its full contents in Cree and English. Cree sentences were paired with their English equivalents on the sentence level on alternating lines. Thus, each original file in the corpus consists of a first line specifying the source URL, followed by the first sentence of the text in English, followed by the corresponding sentence in Cree, followed by an empty line, and so on. For instances in which a given Cree sentence did not have an equivalent in the English version, or vice versa, multiple sentences were given on a single line until a single discursively equivalent section of text could be represented on the respective English and Cree lines. A sample of text taken from the file *GC-030413b* in the corpus is presented below:

>https://publications.gc.ca/site/eng/9.832601/publication.html

Important: This document is for reference purposes only.
mistēyihtākwan: *ōma* masinahikan ta-mosci-wāpahtamihk poko.

These files were then converted into a VRT (vertical) format (Evert and Hardie 2011), with the primary metadata identifiers (e.g., subcorpus, file, and URL) rendered in

XML markup, and the (manually aligned) English and Cree matching passages represented as paragraphs (<p id= . . . >). Cree passages were partitioned into constituent sentences (<s id= . . . >), with the Cree sentences/phrases finally being tokenized into words and punctuation, with each token on its own line. For example:

```
<corpus title="Government-of-Canada-Documents"> [CORPUS TITLE]
. . .
<text file="GC-030413b.txt"> [NAME OF TEXT FILE]
<url="https://publications.gc.ca/site/eng/9.832601/publication.html"> [SOURCE URL]
<p id=1> [CREE-ENGLISH SENTENCE PAIR START]
<crk>mistēyihtākwan: ōma masinahikan ta-mosci-wāpahtamihk poko.</crk> [CREE]
<eng>Important: This document is for reference purposes only.</eng> [ENGLISH]
<s id=1> [TOKENIZED CREE WORDS START]
mistêyihtâkwan [TOKENIZED CREE WORDS]
:
ôma
masinahikan
ta-mosci-wâpahtamihk
poko
.
</s> [TOKENIZED CREE WORDS END]
</p> [CREE-ENGLISH SENTENCE PAIR END]
. . .
</text> [FILE END]
```

Metadata

Each text source in the corpus is named according to its subcorpus and its date of creation using the formula SC-DDMMYY. For instance, a file belonging to the Governmental Texts subcorpus created on the 28th of February, 2023, would receive the name GC-280223. If no date of creation could be established, the file was instead named SC-1, with the next text in the same subcorpus with no known date being SC-2, and so on. Aside from the information contained in the filename, other metadata for each individual source is stored in an external spreadsheet, listing all constituent files by name, providing the original source URL of the relevant text, a link to a formatted and parallelized .txt copy of the text, its date of creation, its genre, its author, the author's place of origin, age at the time of writing, date of birth, the relevant subcorpus, the original language of the text (be it a Cree original or a Cree translation of an English text), and a number representing how closely (in the first author's opinion) the orthography used in the text resembles the SRO on a scale of 1 to 4 (whereby 4 represents perfect SRO, 3 represents SRO with some idiosyncratic elements, 2 represents a mostly idiosyncratic orthography that follows some SRO tenets, and 1 represents an entirely idiosyncratic orthography).

While full metadata can be given for all of the texts in the PED subcorpus and virtually all texts in CLN, GC and MISC both contain a large number of texts with incomplete metadata, particularly concerning the author(s). GC in particular almost never provides any information concerning the author/translator of each text, instead simply labeling each text as being produced by the relevant organ of state. Texts in MISC produced by large corporations often follow suit, as do short, ephemeral texts, such as posters or flyers. In total, 89 files (92.7%) in GC lack any credited author (and thus all authorial metadata), as did 73 files (32.7%) in MISC.

Availability

The MCT corpus and its accompanying metadata sheet will be made available for noncommercial research use with the freely accessible online concordancer Korp (Borin et al. 2012) (https://korp.altlab.app/), with each subcorpus formatted as a .vrt (vertical format) file containing all constituent source texts (as outlined above). Although these source texts are derived from existing, publicly accessible materials, we are nonetheless in the process of verifying usage permissions with the original authors of each constituent source, when they can be reached, and have a framework in place to either entirely remove or render as a nonconsecutive bag-of-words any file in the corpus, if necessary.

Statistics

In total, MCT consists of 559,016 tokens. Excluding punctuation, this can be divided into 280,174 word-form tokens in English, and 193,199 word-form tokens in Cree, representing 61,006 Cree word-form types overall. As such, MCT is well over twice the size of the largest previously existing corpus (AW) and nearly doubles the total token count of all Plains Cree corpora from ~220,000 to ~410,000. Using an existing Plains Cree morphological analyzer (Snoek et al. 2014; Harrigan et al. 2017) and disambiguator (Schmirler et al. 2018; Schmirler 2022), we were able to morphologically analyze and lemmatize 141,163 of the 193,199 nonpunctuation tokens in MCT (73.1%), representing 28,544 Cree word-form types and 6,333 lemma types; of these lemma types, 2,719 also occurred in AW, 2,048 also occurred in BF, and 1,507 occurred in AW, BF, and SD, whereas 3,006 were entirely novel. The 52,036 nonpunctuation tokens that could not be analyzed represented 23,345 types, of which 18,010 (77.1%) were hapax legomena, and only 641 (2.7%) occurred ten or more times overall. In future, it is our plan to manually review and annotate these unrecognized word types (in order of frequency) to determine which among them are genuinely novel and undocumented lexemes, and which are simply evading analysis for orthographic reasons.

Limitations

Although significantly larger in sheer token size than AW, BF, ED, and SD, MCT is not without limitations. Perhaps the most glaring of these is its incomplete metadata; in total, 168 of the 553 texts comprising the corpus have no attributed author, making fine-grained distinctions based on age, region, and fluency impossible to firmly establish, in addition to preventing us from fully providing well-deserved credit to the appropriate authors of each constituent text (particularly in the GC and MISC subcorpora). As such, one of the principal facets of future developments for MCT is the investigation of texts with no current authorial information, facilitated through individually contacting the publishing institution(s) of each such text in order to find this information where possible.

MCT is also subject to orthographic limitations. Unlike existing Plains Cree corpora, all of which are rendered in the SRO, the texts in this corpus are written in an assortment of idiosyncratic orthographies, complicating the matter of searching for exhaustive lists of specific Cree terms. In total, 95 texts representing 77,919 Cree tokens (40.3%) are written in a manner not deemed fully SRO compliant (that is, with an SRO ranking in the metadata of less than 4), with this variation also artificially inflating the type-token ratio of each constituent subcorpus, as certain orthographic variants of the same word form may be counted as separate types. Although there are certain respects in which this orthographic diversity may be of academic use—namely, the lack of consistency in spelling system provides a more accurate descriptive reflection of the manner in which Plains Cree is actually written by the general populace in the present day—the creation of a fully standardized parallel version of this miscellaneous corpus is nonetheless an obvious path for future research.

A final, similar limitation lies in the nature of the constituent texts themselves, namely, 232 texts, representing 41.9% of the total texts and 80.4% of the total Cree token count, are simply Plains Cree translations of texts originally composed in English, rather than natively Cree language data. As such, a large portion of the texts in this corpus may give as much of a reflection of how English is translated into Cree as they do an accurate reflection of Cree-specific phenomena found in more naturalistic, first-hand language production, and may not fully demonstrate the linguistic richness of the target language, as has been noted crosslinguistically in other bodies of translated writing (Baker 2007). Although certainly still useful from a descriptive perspective, given that such a sizable volume of existing written Plains Cree consists simply of translations of English texts to begin with, the translated nature of much of this corpus does render considerable amounts of its data less useful to those studying strictly language internal phenomena.

Potential Use Case

Although perhaps less useful for studying spontaneous or semi-spontaneous L1 Cree speech, one possible task for which this corpus is uniquely well suited is that of terminology development. Plains Cree, like many Indigenous languages, lacks widely accepted technical terminology for many novel technologies, legal concepts, and scientific ideas. One common means of remedying these holes in the lexicon is through terminology development workshops, whereby linguists, domain-relevant experts, and native speakers of the language convene and, through mutual discussion, create a basis of (previously nonexistent) vocabulary for a given (typically socioculturally novel) topic in the language. To this end, MCT contains a large number of translations of technical texts discussing precisely such ideas, particularly those found in the GC and MISC subcorpora, in which the translators have already coined ad hoc in-language neologisms, absent from existing dictionaries, for many of the concepts being discussed. As such, since each text in the corpus has been parallelized on the sentence level with its English equivalent, one needs only search a relevant piece of technical terminology in English to find a Cree sentence containing its translated equivalent. For example, translations for the English term "climate change" are entirely absent from any contemporary Plains Cree dictionary. However, given the large number of modern, environmentally oriented texts present in the MCT corpus, searching "climate change" in MCT yields 34 total results, including numerous neologistic translations:

> Today it's made her one of Canada's leading **climate change** campaigners and the host of Power to the People.
> anohc ekwa nawac nekanestam Canada **petos isaywin** [*sic*] ekwa wehewew anta cakastepayiwinih Power to the People.
> (https://powertothepeople.tv/cr/little-buffalo/)
>
> The GNWT has made progress on **climate change** policy and action planning.
> ôma GNWT osehtawin ka nikânehk *ôma* **ka siwepahk meskocipayiwin** tansi kesehcikewnehk mîna ka tôtamihk oyeyihcikewina [*sic*]
> (https://www.ecc.gov.nt.ca/en/services/nwt-environmental-audit/2020-nwt-environmental-audit)
>
> These quality changes along with declining trends in water quantity, as well as the impacts of **climate change**, exacerbate the potential for ongoing cumulative effects to the watershed and its people.
> Ôhi ayiwâkan mêskocipayiwina sisonê nîhc-âyihk ka-itahkamikahk isi iyikohk nipiy, asici mîna âyimihowin **sisikoc-isiwêpan mêskwacipayiwin** ohci, itocikêmakan nîkânihk kiki âhkami mâwasakonikêwin âyimihowina isi akâmi-sîpîhk êkwa otayisiyinîma.
> (https://www.canada.ca/en/environment-climate-change/services/managing-pollution/sources-industry/mining-effluent/oil-sands/crown-indigenous-working-group-engagement-cr.html)

From this small excerpt alone, three separate attested Plains Cree neologisms for "climate change" can be extracted:

> pîtos isi-ayâwin (originally rendered petos isaywin)—Lit. 'different state of being'
> ka-isiwêpahk mêskocipayiwin (originally rendered ka siwepahk meskocipayiwin)—Lit. 'there will be a change in weather'
> sisikoc-isiwêpan mêskwacipayiwin—Lit. 'there is a sudden change in weather'

Through even simple searches such as this, the MCT corpus can be used to construct an advisory baseline for terminology development, with existing Cree translations of English technical terms being located beforehand by linguists and subsequently proposed as options to fluent speakers and experts, rather than needing to begin discussion for each term from scratch. In addition to this terminological usage, the sentential parallelization of this corpus also lends itself to use as a naturalistic source for example sentences; for instance, rather than creating novel example sentences from scratch for every entry in a dictionary, one could manually or programmatically extract all sentences containing any given Cree word, in addition to the sentence's English translation, from the contents of the corpus. This functionality could also be extended to the improvement of independent computer assisted language learning tools (e.g., Bontogon et al. 2018), where learners could be paired to a relevant corpus text, or given sentences from such a text, as practice exercises, based on the lexical contents of a given lesson.

Conclusion

The MCT corpus represents a substantial addition to the body of available corpus resources in Plains Cree. Despite consisting entirely of existing, publicly available written materials, the compilation of this corpus is the first time that such extant resources have been centralized, categorized, and formatted into a single, searchable database, with this database nearly doubling the total token count of Plains Cree corpora to over 400,000. Although lacking some of the metalinguistic refinements of other corpora, such as orthographic standardization and consistent, thorough metadata, the MCT corpus is unique in its representation not only of Cree translations of English texts (which are only sparsely represented in other corpora), but also in its preponderance of specialized technical documents in fields such as finance, law, medicine, and politics. In this way, the MCT corpus has significant potential as a resource for terminology development, as well as for more conventional linguistic analysis through its large token count and varied composition in genre.

REFERENCES

Ahenakew, Freda. 1987. *Stories of the House People*. Publications of the Algonquian Text Society. Winnipeg: University of Manitoba Press.

Alberta Education. 2009. *Cree Language and Culture: 12-year Program Guide to Implementation*. https://education.alberta.ca/media/563938/cree-12y-guide-to-implementation-k-3.pdf.

Arppe, Antti, Katherine Schmirler, Atticus G. Harrigan, and Arok Wolvengrey. 2020. A Morphosyntactically Tagged Corpus for Plains Cree. *Papers of the Forty-Ninth Algonquian Conference*, ed. by Monica Macaulay and Margaret Noodin, pp. 1–16. East Lansing: Michigan State University Press.

Arppe, Antti, Andrew Neitsch, Daniel Dacanay, Jolene Poulin, Daniel Hieber, and Atticus Harrigan. 2023a. Finding Words that Aren't There: Using Word Embeddings to Improve Dictionary Search for Low-resource Languages. *Proceedings of the Workshop on Natural Language Processing for Indigenous Languages of the Americas (AmericasNLP)*, ed. by Manuel Mager, Abteen Ebrahimi, Arturo Oncevay, Enora Rice, Shruti Rijhwani, Alexis Palmer, and Katharina Kann, pp. 144–155. Toronto: Association for Computational Linguistics. https://aclanthology.org/2023.americasnlp-1.15/.

Arppe, Antti, Atticus G. Harrigan, Katherine Schmirler, Daniel Dacanay, and Rose Makinaw. 2023b. Nêhiyawi-pîkiskwêwina maskwacîsihk: Spoken Dictionary of Maskwacîs Cree. *Dictionaries: Journal of the Dictionary Society of North America* 44(2):127–142. https://doi.org/10.1353/dic.2023.a915068.

Baker, Mona. 2007. Patterns of Idiomaticity in Translated vs. Non-Translated Text. *Belgian Journal of Linguistics* 21(1):11–21. https://doi.org/10.1075/bjl.21.02bak.

Bird, Benjamin, William Charles, and Isaac Bird. 1888. [Letter to Edgar Dewdney] Library and Archives Canada (LAC, RG 10 Vol. 3601, File 1754), Ottawa, Canada.

Bloomfield, Leonard. 1930. *Sacred Stories of the Sweet Grass Cree*. Ottawa: National Museum of Canada Bulletin.

Bloomfield, Leonard. 1934. *Plains Cree Texts*. Publications of the American Ethnological Society 16. New York: G. E. Stechert.

Bontogon, Megan, Antti Arppe, Lene Antonsen, Dorothy Thunder, and Jordan Lachler. 2018. Intelligent Computer Assisted Language Learning (ICALL) for nêhiyawêwin: An In-Depth User-Experience Evaluation. *Canadian Modern Language Review* 74(3):337–362. https://

doi.org/10.3138/cmlr.4054.

Borin, Lars, Markus Forsberg, and Johan Roxendal. 2012. Korp—the Corpus Infrastructure of Språkbanken. *Proceedings of the Eighth International Conference on Language Resources and Evaluation* (*LREC'12*), ed. by Nicoletta Calzolari, Khalid Choukri, Thierry Declerck, Mehmet Uğur Doğan, Bente Maegaard, Joseph Mariani, Asuncion Moreno, Jan Odijk, and Stelios Piperidis, pp. 474–478. Istanbul: European Language Resources Association (ELRA). https://aclanthology.org/L12-1098/.

Brixey, Jacqueline, Eli Pincus, and Ron Artstein. 2018. Chahta Anumpa: A Multimodal Corpus of the Choctaw Language. *Proceedings of the Eleventh International Conference on Language Resources and Evaluation* (*LREC 2018*), ed. by Nicoletta Calzolari, Khalid Choukri, Christopher Cieri, Thierry Declerck, Sara Goggi, Koiti Hasida, Hitoshi Isahara, Bente Maegaard, Joseph Mariani, Hélène Mazo, Asuncion Moreno, Jan Odijk, Stelios Piperidis, and Takenobu Tokunaga, pp. 3371–3376. Istanbul: European Language Resources Association (ELRA). https://aclanthology.org/L18-1532/.

Davies, Mark. 2011. Corpus of American Soap Operas. https://www.english-corpora.org/soap/.

Davies, Mark. 2016. NOW Corpus (News on the Web). https://www.english-corpora.org/now/.

Ellis, C. Douglas 1973. A Proposed Standard Roman Orthography for Cree. *Western Canadian Journal of Anthropology* 3(4):1–37.

Evert, Stefan, and Andrew Hardie. 2011. Twenty-first Century Corpus Workbench: Updating a Query Architecture for the New Millennium. *International Journal of Corpus Linguistics* 17(3):380–409.

Gutierrez-Vasques, Ximena, Gerardo Sierra, and Isaac Hernandez-Pompa. 2016. Axolotl: A Web Accessible Parallel Corpus for Spanish-Nahuatl. *Proceedings of the Tenth International Conference on Language Resources and Evaluation* (*LREC'16*), ed. by Nicoletta Calzolari, pp. 4210–4214. Istanbul: European Language Resources Association (ELRA).

Harrigan, Atticus G., Katherine Schmirler, Antti Arppe, Lene Antonsen, Trond Trosterud, and Arok Wolvengrey. 2017. Learning from the Computational Modeling of Plains Cree Verbs. *Morphology* 27(4):565–598. https://doi.org/10.1007/s11525-017-9315-x.

Harrigan, Atticus, Timothy Mills, and Antti Arppe. 2019. A Preliminary Plains Cree Speech Synthesizer. *Proceedings of the 3rd Workshop on the Use of Computational Methods in the Study of Endangered Languages* (*ComputEL-3*), ed. by Antti Arppe, Jeff Good, Mans Hulden, Jordan Lachler, Alexis Palmer, Lane Schwartz, and Miikka Silfverberg, pp. 64–73. Honolulu: Association of Computational Linguistics. https://journals.colorado.edu/index.php/computel/article/view/421.

Joanis, Eric, Rebecca Knowles, Roland Kuhn, Samuel Larkin, Patrick Littel, Chi-kiu Lo, Darlene Stewart, and Jeffrey Micher. 2020. The Nunavut Hansard Inuktitut–English Parallel

Corpus 3.0 with Preliminary Machine Translation Results. *Proceedings of the Twelfth Language Resources and Evaluation Conference*, ed. by Nicoletta Calzolari, pp. 2562–2572. Istanbul: European Language Resources Association (ELRA).

Lacombe, Albert. 1874. *Dictionnaire de la Langue des Cris*. Montreal: Beauchemin et Valois.

Maheshwari, Anant, Léo Bouscarrat, and Paul Cook. 2018. Towards Language Technology for Mi'kmaq. *Proceedings of the Eleventh International Conference on Language Resources and Evaluation* (*LREC 2018*), ed. by Nicoletta Calzolari, Khalid Choukri, Christopher Cieri, Thierry Declerck, Sara Goggi, Koiti Hasida, Hitoshi Isahara, Bente Maegaard, Joseph Mariani, Hélène Mazo, Asuncion Moreno, Jan Odijk, Stelios Piperidis, and Takenobu Tokunaga, pp. 4139–4143. Istanbul: European Language Resources Association (ELRA). https://aclanthology.org/L18-1653/.

Murdoch, John. 1981. Syllabics—a Successful Educational Innovation. MA thesis, University of Manitoba.

Okimāsis, Jean, and Arok Wolvengrey. 2008. *How to Spell It in Cree* (*The Standard Roman Orthography*). Regina: Miywāsin Ink. https://creeliteracy.org/wp-content/uploads/2016/01/htsiic-covers-nocontacts.pdf.

Pentland, David. 1977. *A Proposed Standard Roman Orthography for Cree*. Regina: Saskatchewan Indian Federated College.

Poulin, Jolene, Daniel Dacanay, and Antti Arppe. 2023. Speech Database (Speech-DB)—An On-Line Platform for Recording, Storing, Validating, and Searching Spoken Language Data. *Proceedings of the Second Workshop on NLP Applications to Field Linguistics*, ed. by Oleg Serikov, pp. 30–39. Dubrovnik: Association for Computational Linguistics. https://aclanthology.org/2023.fieldmatters-1.4.pdf.

Schmirler, Katherine. 2022. Syntactic Features and Text Types in 20th Century Plains Cree: A Constraint Grammar Approach. PhD thesis, University of Alberta. https://doi.org/10.7939/r3-pz87-ye25.

Schmirler, Katherine, Antti Arppe, Trond Trosterud, and Lene Antonsen. 2018. Building a Constraint Grammar Parser for Plains Cree Verbs and Arguments. *Proceedings of the Eleventh International Conference on Language Resources and Evaluation* (*LREC 2018*), ed. by Nicoletta Calzolari, Khalid Choukri, Christopher Cieri, Thierry Declerck, Sara Goggi, Koiti Hasida, Hitoshi Isahara, Bente Maegaard, Joseph Mariani, Hélène Mazo, Asuncion Moreno, Jan Odijk, Stelios Piperidis, and Takenobu Tokunaga, pp. 2981–2988. Istanbul: European Language Resources Association (ELRA). https://aclanthology.org/L18-1472/.

Snoek, Conor, Dorothy Thunder, Kaidi Lõo, Antti Arppe, Jordan Lachler, Sjur Moshagen, and Trond Trosterud. 2014. Modeling the Noun Morphology of Plains Cree. *Proceedings of the 2014 Workshop on the Use of Computational Methods in the Study of Endangered*

Languages, ed. by Jeff Good, Julia Hirschberg, and Owen Rambow, pp. 34–42. Baltimore: Association for Computational Linguistics.

Teodorescu, Daniela, Josie Matalski, Delaney Lothian, Denilson Barbosa, Carrie Demmans-Epp. 2022. Cree Corpus: A Collection of nêhiyawêwin Resources. *Proceedings of the 60th Annual Meeting of the Association for Computational Linguistics (Volume 1: Long Papers)*, ed. by Smaranda Muresan, Preslav Nakov, and Aline Villavicencio, pp. 6354–6364. Dublin: Association for Computational Linguistics. https://aclanthology.org/2022.acl-long.440.

Wolfart, H. Christoph. 1973. Plains Cree: A Grammatical Study. *Transactions of the American Philosophical Society* 63(5):1–90.

Wolvengrey, Arok. 2011. *Cree: Words*. Regina: University of Regina Press.

Zhang, Shiyue, Benjamin Frey, and Mohit Bansal. 2020. ChrEn: Cherokee-English Machine Translation for Endangered Language Revitalization. *Proceedings of the 2020 Conference on Empirical Methods in Natural Language Processing (EMNLP)*, ed. by Bonnie Webber, Trevor Cohn, Yulan He, and Yang Liu, pp. 577–595. Baltimore: Association for Computational Linguistics. https://aclanthology.org/2020.emnlp-main.43/.

Prenominal vs. Postnominal Relative Clauses in Meskwaki

Amy Dahlstrom

The present paper investigates an issue of word order variation in Meskwaki occurring within a noun phrase.[1] Specifically, if a noun is modified by a relative clause, does the relative clause appear before the head noun that it modifies, or after the head noun? I argue here that the unmarked position for relative clauses is postnominal, after the head noun, but that there are at least two motivations for putting a relative clause in the prenominal position. One significant factor favoring the prenominal position involves the information-structural notion of ACTIVATION (Chafe 1994; Lambrecht 1994). Another factor is a syntactic one: if a syntactically complex phrase containing a relative clause functions as a quantifier it is also very likely to appear before the head noun, matching the unmarked position for simple quantifiers. Examples in this paper are drawn from a large corpus of narrative texts written in the early 20th century in the Great Lakes syllabary by monolingual Meskwaki speakers, stored at the National Anthropological Archives of the Smithsonian Institution. The size of the corpus affords us an opportunity to investigate the discourse context of prenominal vs. postnominal relative clauses and to test the usefulness of various information structural factors.

The paper is organized as follows: I first briefly describe the morphosyntax of Meskwaki relative clauses and present examples of the unmarked order of the relative clause following the head noun. The information structure notion of activation is then explained, and contrasted with a different relationship within information structure, that of DEFINITENESS. We will see that the activation status of ACCESSIBILITY is useful for understanding many of the examples of prenominal relative clauses and consider the question of how long the status of accessibility lasts. We then examine a different motivation for placing a relative clause in prenominal position, the syntactically complex quantifier phrases. In the final section I point out a remaining puzzle involving the titles of stories in the Meskwaki syllabic corpus.

Formation of Relative Clauses in Meskwaki

I begin by reviewing how relative clauses are formed in Meskwaki. Meskwaki relative clauses contain a verb inflected in the CONJUNCT PARTICIPLE mode, where the ablaut rule of INITIAL CHANGE applies to the vowel of the first syllable of the verb and in which the conjunct suffix expressing the argument(s) of the relative clause verb is followed by a final suffix of the verb that agrees with the head of the relative clause in gender, number, and obviation, as seen in the schema in (1):

(1) INITIAL CHANGE + **Stem** + Subject.(&.object).agreement + Head.agreement

- INITIAL CHANGE changes a short vowel in the first syllable:

  {a, e, i} → *e·*

  o → *we·*

  Long vowels remain long
- Head agreement suffixes:

  -a proximate animate singular

  -iki proximate animate plural

  -ini obviative animate singular; inanimate plural

  -ihi obviative animate plural

  -i inanimate singular; oblique head

For example, in (2) the conjunct participle *me·hkate·wi·ta* 'one who is fasting' is formed from the verb stem *mahkate·wi·-* 'fast' as follows: Initial change changes the vowel of the first syllable to long *e·*. The suffix *-t* indicates that the subject of 'fast' is third person proximate animate singular. The final suffix *-a* indicates that the head of the relative clause is third person proximate animate singular and is thus coreferential to the subject of the lower verb 'fast'. (Note that in examples (2–4) the individual inflectional morphemes are each given a gloss, to explain the formation of relative clause inflection; later examples do not decompose the individual morphemes and instead give an overall gloss for the categories expressed by the inflectional morphemes as a whole.)[2]

(2) me·hkate·wi·ta
IC-mahkate·wi·-t-a
IC-fast-3-PROX.ANIM.SG.HEAD
'one who is fasting'

One quirk of relative clause formation in Meskwaki is seen when the head of a relative clause is coreferential to an oblique argument expressing stationary location in the lower clause. In such cases the aorist prefix *e·h-* appears on the left edge of the relative clause verb, instead of initial change:

(3) e·howi·kiwa·či
e·h-owi·ki-wa·t-i
AOR-dwell.there-3P-LOC.OBL.HEAD
'the place where they live'

Participles like the one in (2) may be used on their own, or with only a preceding demonstrative, but I focus here on participles that co-occur with an overt head noun (e.g., *oškinawe·ha* 'young man'). Both orders of participle and head noun are robustly attested in texts.

(4) a. PRENOMINAL relative clause:
me·hkate·wi·ta oškinawe·ha
IC-mahkate·wi·-t-a oškinawe·h-a
IC-fast-3-ANIM.SG.HEAD young.man-ANIM.SG
'fasting young man'

b. POSTNOMINAL relative clause:
oškinawe·ha me·hkate·wi·ta
oškinawe·h-a IC-mahkate·wi·-t-a
young.man-ANIM.SG IC-fast-3-ANIM.SG.HEAD
'young man who is fasting'

Unmarked Position for Relative Clauses is Postnominal

I will begin the analysis of relative clause syntax by claiming that the unmarked position for a relative clause is postnominal, to the right of the head noun. This is in contrast to other modifiers, such as demonstratives (e.g., *ma·haki* 'these (animate)') or quantifiers (e.g., *ma·ne* 'many'), whose unmarked position is to the left of the head noun, as seen in the schema in (5).[3]

(5) [Demonstrative Quantifier Noun Relative.clause $]_{NP}$

Restrictive Relative Clauses

We will begin by examining restrictive relative clauses. Examples of postnominal relative clauses can be seen in (6–8), where the relative clause is in boldface:

(6) nešiwikiwa·na maneto·se·ha **ki·wi–so·kenata!**
nešiwiki-wa=i·na maneto·se·h-a IC-**ki·wi–so·ken-ata!**
be.terrible-3.IND=that.ANIM insect-SG IC-around–hold.in.hand-2>3.PART.3
'That bug **you are going around holding in your hand** is terrible!' W58

(7) e·hša·kwe·nemoniči kekimesi **i·nahi we·wi·kiničihi.**
e·h-ša·kwe·nemo-niči kekimesi [**i·nahi** IC-**owi·ki-ničihi**]
AOR-be.unwilling-3'.AOR everyone there IC-dwell.there-3'.PART.3'P
'Everyone **who lived there** didn't want to [go].' W264

(8) nekoti kehči–ma·wa·ka·ni **e·hma·nwikamikesiniči aša·hahi**
nekoti kehči–ma·wa·ka·n-i [**e·h-ma·nwikamikesi-niči** **aša·h-ahi**]
one great-winter.camp-SG AOR-have.many.houses-3'.PART.LOC Sioux-OBV.PL
'It was at a big winter-camp **where the Sioux (obv) had many houses.**'
(Dahlstrom 2015:145)

In (6) the head noun *maneto·se·ha* 'insect' is coreferential to the object of the relative clause, while in (7) the head noun *kekimesi* 'everyone' is coreferential to the subject of the relative clause. In example (8) the head noun *kehči–ma·wa·ka·ni* 'big winter-camp' is coreferential to the oblique argument of the relative clause; because the oblique expresses the semantic relation of stationary location, the aorist prefix *e·h-* appears instead of the usual initial change process affecting the vowel of the leftmost syllable.

The relative clauses in (6–8) are the RESTRICTIVE type of relative clauses: that is, the modifying clause restricts the possible set of referents of the head noun. For example, in (7) the head noun is *kekimesi* 'everyone', but the relative clause restricts the reference of 'everyone' to the individuals who 'live there'.

Nonrestrictive Relative Clauses

Meskwaki also uses conjunct participle verb forms for NONRESTRICTIVE relative clauses: a relative clause that occurs in apposition to a noun phrase. The unmarked position for nonrestrictive relative clauses is also to the right of the noun phrase:[4]

(9) manani·hka ko·hkomesena·na **a·mi–nana·tohtawakwa.**
mana=ni·hka ke-o·hkomes-ena·n-a **IC-a·mi–nana·tohtaw-akwa.**
this.ANIM=MAN'S.EXPL 2-grandmother-21-SG IC-could-ask-21>3.PART.3
'Here's our grandmother, **who we could ask.**' W265

In (9) the bolded clause is not a restrictive relative clause: in other words, it is not defining a restricted subset of 'our grandmothers'. Rather, it is just expressing some additional information about a single individual, the speaker's grandmother.

Example (10) provides an additional illustration of a postnominal nonrestrictive relative clause:

(10) o·ni kehči–maneto·wa **ahpemeki e·wita** e·hnepa·či,
o·ni kehči–maneto·w-a [**ahpemeki IC-awi-ta**] e·h-nepa·-či,
and great–spirit-SG up.aloft IC-be.there-3.PART.3 AOR-sleep-3.AOR
'And while the Great Spirit, **who is up above,** was sleeping,' W308

In the long Wisahkeha text, Wisahkeha's friend, the Great Spirit, is often referred to along with the epithet 'the one who is above' in postnominal position. It is clear that there is only a single individual known as the Great Spirit, so the information about where the Great Spirit is located is not a restrictive relative clause. The fact that nonrestrictive relative clauses also appear to the right of the noun phrase they are associated with strengthens the argument that the postnominal position is the unmarked choice for relative clauses of all types.

Parallel with Complement Clauses

The word order pattern illustrated in (6–10) is parallel to what is found with complement clauses. The unmarked position for a complement clause is to the right of the verb:[5]

(11) ke·htena·peh i·ne·hša·kwe·nemoya·ni **wi·hašihto·ya·ni**
ke·htena=a·peh i·ni=e·h-ša·kwe·nemo-ya·ni **wi·h-ašiht-o·ya·ni**
truly=usually then=AOR-be.unwilling-1.AOR FUT-make-1>0.AOR
'To tell the truth, I then wouldn't want **to make them** [woven bags].' (Goddard 2006:25)

(12) e·hkohtaminiči **i·tepi wi·ha·niči**
e·h-koht-aminiči [**i·tepi wi·h-a·-niči**]
AOR-fear-3′>0.AOR there FUT-go.thither-3′.AOR
'He (obv) was afraid **to go there**.' W312

Although the syntactic roles played by relative clauses and complement clauses are different—relative clauses are modifiers while complement clauses are arguments—they are both syntactically complex elements that may be easier to process occurring toward the end of the higher clause. Indeed, crosslinguistically it is frequently the case that clausal and other 'heavy' constituents appear toward the end of the clause.

Accessibility vs. Definiteness

Before turning to examples of Meskwaki relative clauses occurring in the marked prenominal position, I will briefly review two phenomena of information structure. I first explain what I mean by the term 'accessibility' and then contrast that notion with the separate phenomenon of definiteness.

Accessibility

I argue in this paper that one factor favoring prenominal position for a relative clause is ACCESSIBILITY. Accessibility refers to a property in information structure, part of a larger notion that Chafe 1994 and Lambrecht 1994 call ACTIVATION. (Another name for activation is given (or old) information vs. new information.)

As Chafe (1994) defines it, activation has to do with the speaker's assessment of what is active in the consciousness of the addressee and the speaker's subsequent packaging of the information to align with that assessment.

There are three different assessments that the speaker might make regarding activation. If the speaker believes that a certain piece of information is already active in the addressee's consciousness, the speaker will encode that information as GIVEN. For example, if a particular referent is already being talked about, the speaker is likely to refer to him/her with a weakly accented pronoun or zero anaphora since the speaker can assume that the referent of the pronoun is currently active in the addressee's consciousness. If, on the other hand, the speaker intends to refer to something not connected to the previous context at all, the speaker will encode that information as NEW, assessing that the referent is not active anywhere in the addressee's consciousness. A middle ground is also possible: the speaker may make an assessment that the piece of information in question is ACCESSIBLE. That is, the speaker believes that the information in question is not currently in the addressee's focal consciousness, but may be on the periphery of the addressee's consciousness. What sort of information might be on the periphery of someone's consciousness? The information may be on the periphery because it was mentioned a short while ago (but not in the immediately preceding clause, say), or because it is inferable from the current context. For example, if discussing a wedding, an initial reference to 'the bride' may be considered accessible since the frame evoked by 'wedding' includes participants such as the bride, the groom, etc.

For our purposes here, looking at the information structural properties of relative clauses, the most active state of GIVENNESS is not relevant, since the relative clause appears as an overt item, not a pronoun or zero. Instead, the middle category of ACCESSIBILITY will be useful to us in considering the examples of relative clauses.

Definiteness

In a previous (unpublished) paper on Meskwaki relative clauses, I speculated that the relevant factor determining the word order of head noun and relative clause was definiteness (Dahlstrom 1996b). That turns out not to be the correct analysis, as will be shown below, but I will here briefly define definiteness and contrast it with accessibility.

We saw above that the various statuses of activation are defined in terms of the speaker's assessment of what is active in the addressee's consciousness. The information-structural notion of definiteness, on the other hand, is defined in terms of IDENTIFIABILITY (Chafe 1976:39). That is, if you say *the dog* (as opposed to *a dog*) you are assuming that your addressee can identify the dog in question. Note that even languages lacking a definite article can exhibit an opposition between definite and indefinite: the factor of definiteness could play a role in word order preferences, for example.

The relationship between definiteness and activation may seem a bit confusing at first. Entities marked as definite are often given or accessible, while indefinite entities are often new. However, it is clear that we need to distinguish the two phenomena. A noun phrase marked with a definite article can be new; I could say to my friends, out of the blue, *Hey, you know what? Let's go to the beach!* In such an example *the beach* would be new information (i.e., I assumed that the beach is not active in my friends' consciousness), but it is identifiable, so it is marked with the definite article. The converse situation, for given information to be indefinite, is also possible as shown by an example from Chafe (1976:42) with the pronoun *one*: *I saw an eagle this morning. Sally saw one too.* The use of a pronoun form reflects the given status of the referent, just mentioned in the previous sentence. However, *one* is an indefinite pronoun, not a definite pronoun: the speaker is saying that Sally saw *an eagle* (indefinite), not *the eagle*.

Motivation for a Prenominal Relative Clause: Accessibility

Having defined the concept of accessibility in terms of activation, we can now investigate how the notion of accessibility can be applied to examples of prenominal relative clauses.

Repetition of Predicate

The clearest cases of predicates that the speaker can assume are accessible for the hearer are ones that are an exact repetition of an earlier token of a predicate. For example, in the text published in Dahlstrom 2003, the hero of the story has been blessed by an underwater spirit who has a buffalo head, a reptilian body covered with fish scales, and a rattlesnake tail. After accepting this blessing, the hero is then visited by a second spirit in human form who has wings. The clause in (13) is the first mention of this spirit having wings:

(13) **e·honekwi·kaniniči:**
e·h-onekwi·kani-niči
AOR-have.wings-3'.AOR
'**He (obv) had wings:**' [illustration showing spirit with wings] (Dahlstrom 2003:26)

Example (13) is followed by the winged spirit scolding the hero for accepting the blessing of the underwater spirit. It is a fairly lengthy speech (19 clauses), which is followed by the clause in (14):

(14) "..." e·hikoči i·nini **we·nekwi·kaniničini** neniwani.
"..." e·h-∅-ikoči
AOR-say.thus.to.3'>3.AOR

[i·nini **IC-onekwi·kani-ničini** neniw-ani]
that.OBV IC-have.wings-3'.PART.3' man-OBV
'"..." the man **with wings** (obv) told him.' (Dahlstrom 2003:29)

Example (14) contains a quoting verb and identifies the speaker as 'that man with wings', putting the relative clause to the left of the head noun *neniwani* 'man (obv)'. I suggest that the placement of the relative clause before the head noun is motivated by the author assuming that the predicate is accessible in the consciousness of the hearer/reader of the clause. (Notice that a separate informational-structural notion, CONTRASTIVENESS (Chafe 1976:33; Lambrecht 1994:286), is not the explanation here: the man with wings is not being contrasted with a different man who lacks wings.)

Another example where a prenominal relative clause repeats a verb stem used earlier in the text can be seen in (15–16). First, the Great Spirit and Wisahkeha are described as sitting as two (i.e., sitting together):

(15) **e·hni·šo·piwa·či** wi·sahke·hani,
e·h-ni·šo·pi-wa·či wi·sahke·h-ani,
AOR-sit.as.two-3P.AOR W-OBV
'He [the Great Spirit] and Wisahkeha (obv) were **sitting together**,' W408

A few clauses later, a relative clause formed from the verb *ni·šo·pi-* 'sit as two' appears in prenominal position:

(16) “maniča·hi ma·haki **ni·šo·pičiki** owi·hka·neti·haki ‘. . .’ inenakwe,
“mani=ča·hi ma·haki **IC-ni·šo·pi-čiki** owi·hka·neti·h-aki
now=so these.ANIM IC-sit.as.two-3P.PART.3P friend-PL

‘. . .’ in-enakwe,
say.thus.to-3(P)>21.SUBJUNCT
‘So now, if these friends **sitting together** tell us, “. . .”,’ W409

Since the two characters were just recently described as sitting together, it can be assumed that this description is still accessible in the hearer’s/reader’s consciousness.

Accessibility Is Not Equivalent to Definiteness

It might be thought that the relevant property motivating the appearance of the relative clause in (14) to the left of the head noun is definiteness. After all, the example in (14) is translated with the definite article. In fact, however, definiteness is not the relevant property. Consider the example in (17), from the same text as (13–14). In (17) the underwater spirit blessing the hero predicts he will kill enemy warriors who are famous. The prediction uses the verb *a·čimekosi-* ‘be told about’:[6]

(17) mo·šakike·hmeko e·nemi–**a·čimekosita** i·na wi·hanemi–nesata,
mo·šaki=ke·hi=meko IC-anemi–**a·čimekosi**-ta
only=and=EMPH IC-future–**be.told.about**-3.PART.3

i·na IC-wi·h-anemi–nes-ata,
that IC-FUT-future–kill-2>3.PART.3
‘And only ones who are greatly renowned are who you will kill,’ (Dahlstrom 2003:23)

Later in the story the hero takes part in his first battle. The people he kills are listed, including the warrior described in (18):

(18) o·ni **a·čimekosiničinina**·hkameko kehči–we·ta·se·wani,
o·ni IC-**a·čimekosi**-ničini=na·hka=meko kehči–we·ta·se·w-ani,
and IC-**be.told.about**-3′.PART.3′=also=EMPH great–warrior-OBV
‘and also a great warrior (obv) who was renowned indeed,’ (Dahlstrom 2003:37)

The description of the warrior in (18) uses the predicate *a·čimekosi-* 'be told about', matching the spirit's earlier prediction, and the relative clause appears to the left of the head noun. But notice that (18) is translated with an indefinite article, not a definite article. The individual who was killed by the hero was not mentioned before and therefore is not identifiable to the audience. However, the property of being famous was introduced earlier and is therefore accessible to the listener/reader of the story.

Accessible through Inference

We saw in (13–18) that repetition of the predicate contained in a relative clause can reflect the accessibility of that predicate. Another way that a predicate may have accessible status is if something related to that predicate was mentioned earlier in the context. For example, consider the sentence in (19) in which the author is recounting how her mother taught her to cut and gather firewood:

(19) **e·hmanese·ya·ka**·pehe nekya,
ni·nake·h netanemo·ta **ki·šahama·nini** papi·wi-mese·he·hani

e·h-manese·-ya·ke=a·pehe ne-ky-a,
AOR-cut.firewood-1P.AOR=usually 1-mother-SG

ni·na=ke·h ne-anemo·t-a **IC-ki·šah-ama·nini**
I=moreover 1-carry.along.on.back-1>0.IND IC-chop-1>0.PART.0P

papi·wi-mese·he·h-ani
small–piece.of.firewood-PL
'When my mother and I went to **cut firewood**,
I would carry home on my back the little sticks of wood I **had chopped**.'
(Goddard 2006:23)

In (19) the verb of the first clause, *manese·-* 'cut firewood', evokes a schema of what is involved in obtaining firewood. The verb of the relative clause in the second line, *ki·šah-* 'chop', is therefore accessible to the hearer and appears in prenominal position.

However, not all examples of relative clauses formed from inferable predicates appear in prenominal position. For example, consider the textual excerpt in (20):

(20) o·nipi e·hwe·pi–**a·čimoči** aša·ha e·to·ta·kowa·či i·nini mahkate·wi–anakwe·wani.
e·hma·ne·wa·či neniwaki **pe·seša·čiki.**

o·ni=ipi e·h-we·pi–**a·čimo-či** aša·h-a
and.then=HRSY AOR-begin–narrate-3.AOR Sioux-SG

IC-to·taw-ekowa·či i·nini mahkate·wi–anakwe·w-ani.
IC-treat.so-3′>3P.PART.OBL that.OBV Black–Rainbow-OBV

e·h-ma·ne·-wa·či neniw-aki **IC-peseše·-čiki.**
AOR-be.many-3P.AOR man-PL IC-listen-3P.PART.3P
'And then, they say, the Sioux launched into **his account** of what had been done to them by Black Rainbow (obv).
There were many men **listening.**' (Goddard 2007:188)

The verb in the first line, *a·čimo-* 'narrate', implies that the narrator is speaking to listeners. However, the relative clause in the second line, *pe·seša·čiki* 'ones who were listening', appears after the head noun *neniwaki* 'men', which is the unmarked position for relative clauses.

How Long Does Accessibility Last?

A question asked by Chafe (1976:32) is how long givenness lasts. Chafe points out that there is a limited capacity in consciousness, and that the treatment of an item as given depends upon the speaker's assessment of what the hearer has in his/her consciousness. For the Meskwaki relative clauses we can ask a similar question about accessibility: When might a speaker/author decide that a previously mentioned property is no longer in the addressee's/reader's consciousness at all?

With regard to this question, it is of interest to look at examples of noun phrases containing relative clauses that are introduced with a distal absentative demonstrative. One use of this paradigm of demonstratives is to refer back to a referent mentioned in a previous episode (Goddard 1990:330). The examples I have found in my corpus of relative clauses appearing in noun phrases introduced by a distal absentative demonstrative have all been postnominal. In other words, the reference to an earlier mention of the referent may be too far back for the speaker to assume that the predicate of the relative clause is accessible to the hearer. Example (21) provides an illustration of a previously mentioned character being reintroduced into the story:

(21) keye·hapake·h **i·niya** ihkwe·he·hayo·we **e·ye·h–pwa·wi–ona·pe·miya·ni**
ka·ki·wi·–'te·maka ke·ko·he·nahina·čimoha·tehe

keye·hapa=ke·h [**i·niya** ihkwe·he·h-a=iyo·we
it.turned.out=moreover that.ABSENT woman.DIM-SG=PAST

IC-**aye·hi–pwa·wi–ona·pe·mi-ya·ni** IC-**ka·-ki·wi–wi·te·m-aka**]
IC-continue.to–not–have.husband-1.CC IC-REDUP-around–accompany-1>3.PART.3

ke·ko·hi IC-inah-ina·čimoh-a·tehe
something IC-REDUP-inform.so-3>3'.CH.PRET

'I later found out that **that** young woman **I had gone around with before I got married** had been telling him (obv) tales.' (Goddard 2006:111)

The narrator is referring to a friend from her single days, last mentioned in the story 43 pages earlier. The noun phrase referring to her former friend is introduced with the distal absentative demonstrative *i·niya* 'that (absent)', and the relative clause follows the head noun.

Another Environment Favoring Prenominal Relative Clauses

The information-structural notion of accessibility is not the only reason why a relative clause may occur in the prenominal position. Another motivation for a relative clause appearing before the head noun is a syntactic one: syntactically complex expressions of quantifiers involving relative clauses appear before the head noun, in the same position as a simple quantifier. Example (22) shows that the unmarked position for simple quantifiers is to the left of the head noun:

(22) nekoti ne·sa·wa·čini **ma·ne**meko owi·ya·si wi·hki·šihto·waki,
nekoti IC-nes-a·wa·čini
one IC-kill-3P>3′.ITER

ma·ne=meko owi·ya·s-i wi·h-ki·šiht-o·waki,
much=EMPH meat-SG FUT-finish.making-3P>0.IND
'Whenever they kill one [buffalo] they will make **a lot of** meat.' W452

Now consider the example in (23), in which Wisahkeha is beginning to create the world in which the future humans will live:

(23) o·ni, "***ča·kimeko*** **e·šikekini** maškihkye·ni wi·htakowani," e·hiči.
o·ni, "**ča·ki=meko IC-išiken-kini** maškihky-ani
and.then all=EMPH IC-be.so-0.PART.0P grass-PL

wi·h-tako-wani," e·h-i-či.
FUT-exist-0P.IND AOR-say.thus-3.AOR
'And then he said, "There will exist **all kinds of** grasses."' W310

In (23) the quantifier phrase translated as 'all kinds of' is formed with the inanimate intransitive verb stem *išiken-* 'be so, be of such kind', which takes *ča·ki* 'all' as its oblique argument. The verb stem *išiken-* is inflected as a participle in which the inanimate plural head (agreeing with grasses) is coreferential to the subject of *išiken-*.

Another example of this type may be seen in (24):

(24) **a·čipanakiči e·šikeniki** mi·čiweni wi·hišimeko–mesawinamowa·či e·šina·kwihto·niči.
a·čipanakiči IC-išiken-niki mi·čiwen-i
all.kinds IC-be.so-0′.PART.0 food-SG

IC-wi·h-iši–=meko –mesawin-amowa·či IC-išina·kwiht-o·niči
IC-FUT-thus–=EMPH –like.the.looks.of-3P>0.PART.OBL IC-make.look.so-3′>0.PART.0
'**all kinds of** food which he (obv) made look very tempting to them' W195

In (24) we again see a syntactically complex quantifier phrase translated as 'all kinds of' formed with the verb stem *išiken-* 'be so, be of such kind'. The particle *a·čikpanakiči* 'all kinds' functions as the oblique argument of *išiken-*, which is inflected as a participle with an inanimate head of the relative clause. The relative clause formed from *išiken-* is in prenominal position, parallel to the unmarked position for simple quantifiers.[7]

A Remaining Puzzle

The texts in the Smithsonian corpus generally have titles provided by the writers, and the titles often contain relative clauses.[8] Some of the relative clauses are prenominal, which is surprising given the observations about prenominal relative clauses made above. As (25) shows, some relative clauses in titles are in fact in the unmarked postnominal position:

(25) oškinawe·ha **me·hkate·wi·ta**
oškinawe·h-a **IC-mahkate·wi·-ta**
young.man-SG IC-fast-3.PART.3
'A young man **who fasted**' [= example (4b)] (Dahlstrom 1996a:129)

A postnominal relative clause in a story title is what I would predict, given the analysis in the previous sections of the paper: postnominal is the unmarked position for relative clauses, and there is no prior context that would motivate the author to place the relative clause in prenominal position.

Nevertheless, there are a number of story titles in the National Anthropological Archives corpus in which a prenominal relative clause appears, as in (26):

(26) **me·hkate·wi·ta** našawaye–neniwa
IC-mahkate·wi·-ta našawaye–neniw-a
IC-fast-3.PART.3 long.ago–man-SG
'A man of long ago **who fasted**' (Dahlstrom 2015:134)

The example in (26) forms a near-minimal pair with (25), and it is hard to understand what motivates the difference in word order between the two titles.

Furthermore, (27) demonstrates that even nonrestrictive relative clauses can be prenominal in titles:

(27) **e·sa·mekwama·ta me·neto·wita** sakime·wa
IC-asa·mekwama·-ta IC-maneto·wi-ta sakime·w-a
IC-overfast-3.PART.3 IC-be.spirit-3.PART.3 mosquito-SG
'Mosquito, who fasted too long [and] who became a spirit' (Kiyana 1912, title)

Note that *sakime·wa* 'mosquito' is a personal name for a human character here, so the relative clauses in (27) are clearly the nonrestrictive type. I unfortunately do not have an explanation for why relative clauses in some titles appear in prenominal position, and must leave it as a puzzle for now.[9]

Conclusion

I have argued in this paper that the unmarked position for relative clauses is postnominal, following the head noun, based on the distribution of both restrictive and nonrestrictive relative clauses, and the parallel with the unmarked position of complement clauses. Many examples of prenominal relative clauses can be accounted for by appealing to the information structure notion of accessibility: either the predicate of the relative clause is accessible by repetition of the same predicate, or the predicate is inferable based upon the earlier context. A separate motivation for a relative clause to appear in prenominal position is when the relative clause is part of a syntactically complex quantifier phrase. A remaining puzzle, however, is found in story titles containing a relative clause. The account proposed here would predict that such relative clauses would occur only in the unmarked, postnominal position, since there is no earlier context to make the predicate of the relative clause accessible, but instead titles exhibit both prenominal and postnominal relative clauses.

NOTES

1. Thanks to Lucy Thomason, Erik Gooding, and other members of the audience at the 55th Algonquian Conference, Edmonton, for useful comments and suggestions, as well as to two anonymous reviewers.
2. Abbreviations: 1P = first person exclusive plural, 21 = first person inclusive plural, 3P = third person animate plural, 3′ = animate obviative, 0 = inanimate, 0′ = inanimate obviative, ABSENT = absentative demonstrative, ANIM = animate, AOR = aorist prefix;

aorist conjunct inflection, CC = changed conjunct, CH.PRET = changed preterit, DIM = diminutive, EMPH = emphatic, EXPL = expletive, FUT = future, HRSY = hearsay evidential, IC = initial change (ablaut rule), IND = independent indicative, ITER = iterative, LOC = locative, OBL = oblique head of relative clause, OBV = obviative, PART = conjunct participle, PL = plural, PROX = proximate, REDUP = reduplication, SG = singular, SUBJUNCT = subjunctive. Subject and object features in verb inflection are separated by > and are followed by identification of the verbal paradigm. The head of a relative clause is identified following the label PART (participle). An en-dash (–) indicates a boundary between a preverb and the remainder of the verb, or between a prenoun and a noun stem. Vowel length is marked by a raised dot. Examples cited as W are from Kiyana 1913.

3. Demonstratives and quantifiers may also occur after the head noun; see Goddard and Dahlstrom (2022:250).
4. In other words, the distinction between restrictive and nonrestrictive relative clauses in Meskwaki is a semantic one, not morphological or syntactic.
5. Note, however, that subordinate clauses functioning as oblique arguments to the matrix verb appear to the left of the verb, in the unmarked position for oblique arguments.
6. The final suffixes on the participles are animate singular, but it is clear from the context that this has a collective sense.
7. Note that *mi·čiweni* 'food' in (24) is followed by another relative clause as well, in the unmarked postnominal position.
8. More examples of both prenominal and postnominal relative clauses in titles can be seen in the set of Meskwaki texts uploaded by Ives Goddard and Lucy Thomason: https://repository.si.edu/handle/10088/17270.
9. A suggestion was made in the discussion period that in at least some cases the author may have added the title after completing the story, so that we can't assume that the word order of the title reflects a context in which the information expressed in the relative clause is entirely new. Perhaps this observation helps explain the variation seen in the word order of the titles.

REFERENCES

Chafe, Wallace. 1976. Givenness, Contrastiveness, Definiteness, Subjects, Topics, and Point of View. *Subject and Topic*, ed. by Charles Li, pp. 27–55. New York: Academic Press.

Chafe, Wallace. 1994. *Discourse, Consciousness, and Time: The Flow and Displacement of Conscious Experience in Speaking and Writing.* Chicago: University of Chicago Press.

Dahlstrom, Amy. 1996a. Narrative Structure of a Fox Text. *nikotwâsik iskwâhtêm, pâskihtêpayih!*

Studies in Honour of H. C. Wolfart, ed. by John D. Nichols and Arden C. Ogg, pp. 113–162. Algonquian and Iroquoian Linguistics Memoir 13. Winnipeg: Algonquian and Iroquoian Linguistics.

Dahlstrom, Amy. 1996b. Pragmatic Issues in Fox Relative Clauses. Paper read at the 28th Algonquian Conference, University of Toronto.

Dahlstrom, Amy. 2003. Warrior Powers from an Underwater Spirit: Cultural and Linguistic Aspects of an Illustrated Meskwaki Text. *Anthropological Linguistics* 45(1):1–56.

Dahlstrom, Amy. 2015. Highlighting Rhetorical Structure through Syntactic Analysis: An Illustrated Meskwaki Text by Alfred Kiyana. *New Voices for Old Words: Algonquian Oral Literatures*, ed. by David J. Costa, pp. 118–197. Lincoln: University of Nebraska Press.

Goddard, Ives. 1990. Aspects of the Topic Structure of Fox Narratives: Proximate Shifts and the Use of Overt and Inflectional NPs. *International Journal of American Linguistics* 56(3):317–340.

Goddard, Ives. 2006. *The Autobiography of a Meskwaki Woman: A New Edition and Translation.* Algonquian and Iroquoian Linguistics Memoir 18. Winnipeg: Algonquian and Iroquoian Linguistics.

Goddard, Ives. 2007. *The Owl Sacred Pack: A New Edition and Translation of the Meskwaki Manuscript of Alfred Kiyana.* Algonquian and Iroquoian Linguistics Memoir 19. Winnipeg: Algonquian and Iroquoian Linguistics.

Goddard, Ives, and Amy Dahlstrom. 2022. Meskwaki (Algonquian) Evidence against Basic Word Order and Configurational Models of Argument Roles. *Language Change and Linguistic Diversity: Studies in Honour of Lyle Campbell*, ed. by Thiago Costa Chacon, Nala H. Lee, and W. D. L. Silva, pp. 242–259. Edinburgh: Edinburgh University Press.

Kiyana, Alfred. 1912. *esamegamata menetowita sakimewa.* [Mosquito, Who Fasted Too Long and Became a Spirit.] Manuscript 2984, National Anthropological Archives, Smithsonian Institution, Washington, DC.

Kiyana, Alfred. 1913. *wisakea osani okyeni osimeani okomeseani.* [Wisahkeha, His Father, His Mother, His Younger Brother, His Grandmother.] Manuscript 2958-a, National Anthropological Archives, Smithsonian Institution, Washington, DC.

Lambrecht, Knud. 1994. *Information Structure and Sentence Form: Topic, Focus, and the Mental Representations of Discourse Referents.* Cambridge: Cambridge University Press.

A Divided Tribe Is a Colonized Tribe

Reexamining Meskwaki Patrilineal Tribal Membership (before and after 1937)

Erik D. Gooding and Lily Lee Gooding

On the morning of 8 May 2022, the Meskwaki Settlement awoke to find the question "How can you be proud to be Meskwaki if half the tribe doesn't matter to you?" graffitied on the side of the Meskwaki Tribal Center, and the statement "A divided tribe is a colonized tribe" on a tribal roadway. Later that same day on social media, the same person posted a quote from the Sauk leader Blackhawk: "We are becoming like them, hypocrites and liars, adulterers, lazy drones, all talkers, and no workers." These actions reignited in the Meskwaki community the long-standing tumultuous debate concerning the tribal membership requirement that was enacted on 13 November 1937, following the instigation of the Indian Reorganization Act of 1934, that is based solely on patrilineal descent. This paper explores this requirement, examining evidence of pre-1937 tribal membership ideas, the creation of the requirement in the 1937 Tribal Constitution and the consequences of that decision.[1]

1937 Tribal Constitution

The 1934 passage of the Wheeler-Howard Act, also known as the Indian Reorganization Act (IRA), escalated the changing dynamics of the Meskwaki political system. Up until the death of the last recognized chief, Pushetonequa, the Meskwaki had persisted with a system of leadership based on a hereditary chief leading a clan-based representative council. After Pushetonequa's death in 1919, the local Indian superintendent created and led a new council with five members (down from the previous 12) until a formal elected business council was established through the IRA (Brown 1964; Foley 1995). During this period from 1919 to 1934, Meskwaki factionalism deepened further, splitting the tribe into two factions, each with roots that predate the 20th century: the conservative, *Aškwihuk* 'people lagging behind', and the progressives.[2]

In June 1935 the Meskwaki voted to accept the Howard-Wheeler Act, and the progressive faction, the voting majority at that time, established a new tribal council (Brown 1964). That council created a four-person committee to draft the new tribal constitution, which consisted of progressives Edward Davenport, George Youngbear, Horace Poweshiek, and William Poweshiek (Brown 1964). On 13 November 1937 that new Tribal Constitution was ratified by a tribal vote, 80 votes for to 78 votes against, with 158 voting out of 204 eligible voters at that time (Brown 1964). It included Article II, "Membership," which established the tribal enrollment requirement. It stated that members of the Meskwaki tribe would only be "all persons whose names appear on the official census roll of January 1, 1937, of the Sac and Fox Tribe in Iowa [and . . .] all children born since the completion of said roll whose father is a member" (Meskwaki Nation 1937).[3] Since the inclusion of the patrilineal membership requirement in 1937, tribal members and tribal descendants (those descended from mothers who were tribal members but whose fathers were nonmembers) have questioned the validity and the intent of that decision.

Tribal Membership before 1937

Concerning the validity of the decision, Meskwaki today ask two essential questions: (1) What was the Meskwaki membership requirement before the new constitution? and (2) Why was patrilineal descent chosen as the membership requirement? To address these questions, we need to examine aspects of pre-1937 Meskwaki culture and history, and we will begin with the role of patrilineal descent prior to 1937.

Patrilineal descent appears to play a key role in three principal areas of Meskwaki culture: (1) the assignment of a child into the dual divisions; (2) the assignment of children into a clan; and (3) the use of an Omaha-type kinship system. For the Meskwaki, dual divisions are non-unilineal groups that are not descent groups (Callender 1978a:616–617). Dual divisions, therefore, are "units that crosscut clans, lineages, and families" that are employed to "determine seating and other kinds of placement at some public events, including rituals," and that "provide the basis for opposition and rivalry . . . in games and contests and by prescribed joking across divisional lines" (Callender 1994:108–109). Children are placed into a division based on birth order in relation to the father's dual division membership. The dual divisions among the Meskwaki are the *ki:ško:ha* and *to:hka:na*. The firstborn is assigned to the opposite division of the father: if the father is a *ki:ško:ha*, then the child is a *to:hka:na*; if the father is a *to:hka:na*, the firstborn then is a *ki:ško:ha*. The subsequent children of the father will then alternate. There is no differentiation based on the sex of the child; the only determining factor of assignment is the birth order in relation to the father's division membership.

Clans, in Meskwaki culture, are naming and ritual groups with membership based on patrilineal descent (Jones 1939; Morgan 1964; Callender 1978b). According to Callender:

> Each clan was descended in theory from a person who, seeking a vision, had been blessed by a spirit in the form of the eponym. This original vision included instructions for assembling the pack and directions for its ceremonies as well as its names. Through the names and the pack, the powers of the ancestral vision extended to all members of the clan and could be invoked through pack ritual. (1978b:639)

Clans perform semiannual ceremonies and were also used formerly to regulate marriage (clan exogamy). They were also comprised of lineages, which were used as the "primary vehicle for transmission of hereditary ritual positions and political offices" (Callender 1962:26–28).

Since contact, the names and the numbers of Meskwaki clans have varied (see Thwaites 1896–1901; Forsyth 1912; Michelson 1925; Jones 1939; Tax 1955; Goddard 1975). In Jones (1939), the last chief, Pushetonequa, around 1900 indicated that the

Bear, Fox, Eagle, Thunder, and Wolf were the original Meskwaki clans. Goddard (1975) has argued for the presence of those five clans in the writings of Allouez in 1672, at the time of European contact. The presence of additional clans beyond these "original five" will be addressed below.

The third area within patrilineal descent that outwardly appears to play a prominent role in Meskwaki culture is their kinship system, which has been described as the Omaha system (Michelson 1925; Jones 1939; Tax 1955). The Omaha system is one of four kinship systems employed in Indigenous North America, along with the Crow, Iroquois, and Eskimo (Eggan 1955). Two of these systems, Iroquois and Eskimo, are bilateral, while the remaining two are unilineal, with the Crow the matrilineal system, and the Omaha the patrilineal system. These three areas that rely on patrilineal descent are certainly strong arguments for the importance of patrilineal descent to Meskwaki culture, but do they indicate in any way that tribal membership was based on patrilineal descent? Are there areas of Meskwaki culture that emphasize matrilineal descent, or even bilateral descent?

A survey of historical materials provides no definitive indication that pre-1937 tribal membership was based on patrilineal descent. There are, however, a series of examples that may indicate important roles for either matrilineal or bilateral kinship units, lessen the importance of patrilineal descent, or reduce the perception of male dominance.

Several cultural mechanisms rely on maternal family participation. The first of these is a matrilineal postmarital residence emphasis. Several sources, including "The Autobiography of a Fox Woman" (Michelson 1925) as well as Marston (1912) and Callender (1962), indicate and conclude a preference for matrilocal residence and matrilocal extended families in Meskwaki summer villages. In addition to these, there are also older examples that indicate postmarital residence was matrilocal (Michelson 1925; Callender 1962).

The next area where the matrilineal family serves important roles within the family is in regard to child development. The first is the use of the maternal uncle as a child's disciplinarian or "boogeyman" (Tax 1955). Giving this responsibility to the maternal uncle relieves the parents from this function. The second is the use of the maternal aunt in a position best described as the "relationship checker." That aunt will/should be approached by her niece when the niece has romantic intentions. The aunt's task is to make sure that her niece and the potential suitor are not related. The third area is the practice of the sororate upon the death of a mother. This practice requires for her to be replaced in the marriage by her family with a female family member, preferably sister or cousin (Tax 1955).[4] Meskwaki interpret this practice as prioritizing the needs of the children over the widower, keeping the matrilineal relatives involved in the lives of the children. These matrilineal aspects of Meskwaki culture indicate/illustrate that Meskwaki kinship, even though classified as an Omaha-type kinship system with its perceived patrilineal dominance, recognized the matrilineal side of families and entrusted them with important kinship roles.

The next set of examples concerns the position of patrilineal descent in relation to clans, dual division placement, and the kinship system—the three instances discussed previously in support of the importance of patrilineal descent in Meskwaki culture. Jones, in his discussion of the dual divisions, wrote: "A person is appointed to one or the other division while a young infant. The appointment is made by the father and mother, the father usually having more voice in the matter" (1939:81). The father "usually" having more voice in the matter perhaps signals that the father's choice is not exclusively the factor in dual division assignment. Jones (1939:81) continued: "The regular way is to put the first-born in one class, and the second-born in the other. The rest of the children follow in the same alternation." Again, the expression "regular way" seems to indicate other ways of assignment, and in fact, Jones then mentions the exact opposite when he states that a "father is likely to put the first-born in the class of which he is a member, but it is not necessary for him to do so. He can, if he wishes, make all of his children members of one class" (1939:81). Elders today emphasize the importance of everyone having a dual division assignment and indicate that there are accepted matrilineal mechanisms in place to make that assignment, including the assignment of children from a non-Meskwaki father.

In regard to clans, Tax (1955) described the situation of the Eagle clan, one of the five original clans, during the 1930s. He observed that they had almost died out, and their membership at one point consisted of twelve members with the only male being elderly (1955:265). Yet by the 1950s the Eagle clan had "remained ritually active, maintained as a demographically viable unit by giving Eagle names to persons whose fathers belonged to other clans" (Callender 1994:111). Meskwaki elders today have noted several reasons for not placing a child in the father's clan. The first is if a married couple has had misfortune with previous children named into the father's clan, particularly if the children have had health concerns or if they had died. In this situation, the couple may seek permission to name the child into a different clan. The second is in regard to declining clan membership and is what appears to have happened to the Eagle clan in the 1900s. If a clan is low on members, they can ask to have a newborn named into their clan. A third example is if the child's father is not a member of a clan, either a non-Meskwaki Indigenous person or a non-Indigenous person, then typically a matrilineal elder will name the child to the clan of their choosing. Tax (1955) provides a breakdown of the clan affiliation of the Meskwaki in 1932 that illustrates the use of these alternative naming mechanisms. He noted that of the 366 Meskwaki listed, 71 were named from a clan other than the father's (1955:264).

Concerning the Omaha kinship system, while it is recognized by its use of patrilineal descent, there is, however, variation within the Omaha system by the groups that employ it. Tax (1955), in his analysis of Meskwaki kinship, observed the way Meskwaki actually adapted the system to their culture, noting at times how the Meskwaki strayed from the "classic" Omaha system. In regard to the treatment and feelings toward relatives Tax wrote: "Underlying all patterns of behavior is a general feeling that there should be good will toward all relatives, by marriage as well as by blood" (1955:255). In his discussions of the household or family grouping he observed that "in all cases the family group most meaningful in daily life is absolutely bilateral" (1955:260), and that "the bilateral family is the most important social unit" (1955:261). And in his concluding remarks he commented on the system as a whole, noting that first "the Fox seem to have been developing a system as completely bilateral as possible, notwithstanding its supposedly unilateral Omaha feature" (1955:281), and second, that "the question of how unilateral the Fox kinship system is, is essential to an understanding of the entire question. One has a strong feeling that, even though this type of kinship system is often accompanied by patrilineal groupings, yet the Fox system in practice is as bilateral as any" (1955:281). While patrilineal descent initially appears to play an important role in Meskwaki culture in the areas of dual division, clan membership, and their kinship system, Meskwaki culture appears to allow for other nonpatrilineal-based decisions to be made and nonpatrilineal relationships to be employed and even emphasized.

The next example is in reference to the ability of the Meskwaki to incorporate outsiders throughout history, primarily through "shifts in residence and extensive intermarriage across tribal boundaries" (Callender 1994:110). In the early 1600s, the Meskwaki, Sauk, Kickapoo, and Potawatomi lived in close proximity in lower Michigan and northern Ohio with a high degree of intermarriage and mixed settlements. During this time Claude Jean Allouez noted that the Meskwaki intermingled with the Potawatomi (Thwaites 1896–1901, 51:43). This intermingling continued through the middle of the 1600s following their movement to Wisconsin, as noted by Nicolas Perrot, who also described the Sauk as part Meskwaki (Perrot 1911:270).

In his study on Meskwaki social organization from 1650 to 1850, Goddard (1975) observed the addition of new clans to the "original five" as referenced by Chief Pushetonequa (Jones 1939). Goddard notes that the process of adding clans that began in the 17th century continued through the 19th and 20th centuries, and that it should be "understood as a concomitant of the building of the Fox [Meskwaki] tribes, in part by the in-marrying or adoption of foreign males, after the drastic reduction in population during the wars with the French" (Goddard 1975:137–138). Today Meskwaki elders refer to this process of incorporating outsiders into the tribe as "changing their moccasins."

The final two examples are in regard directly to the role of men and women in politics and religion, and indirectly to the status of men and women throughout Meskwaki culture in general. To outsiders, the Meskwaki historically appear to be a male-dominated society, with men occupying all the political roles from clan leadership to village leadership, as well as tribal leadership. To insiders, the situation is more complicated. Meskwaki culture is comprised of a series of tasks that are required for their continuance. Various mechanisms are in place to assist individuals and groups of Meskwaki to accomplish these tasks. Social statuses and roles were created for this purpose as well, and those positions were assigned to gendered individuals. Outsiders have presumed that Meskwaki value and view certain statuses the same as they do, assigning higher value to certain positions, such as political leadership. However, that is not the case in Meskwaki culture, where the gendered statuses and activities are viewed as complementary, necessary, equally valued parts of the whole. For example, males were historically clan leaders representing their clan on the village council, and outsiders viewed their status as expressing a higher value than females. However, outsiders failed to understand the female's role in selecting and advising (and some would say instructing) their male clan representatives. Religion presents a similar dilemma. Outsiders see again male dominance through leadership positions and ceremonial roles. But there is a Meskwaki saying: "Men can only have visions; it's women who have children and therefore they can make the future." Females have their tasks; males have their tasks. Both are equally valued and necessary for the benefit and survival of the Meskwaki. Outsiders have mistakenly interpreted Meskwaki culture from their own perspective, and their interpretations have often elevated Meskwaki men above Meskwaki women.

In addition to these examples where either patrilineal descent is not as important as it seems to be, or where there is an actual emphasis on the matrilineal side of the family (or bilateral), there are specific examples from throughout Meskwaki history where patrilineal descent does not appear to have been the defining feature of tribal membership. The historic record contains examples of individuals who have been identified as being mixed blood.

We can start with an event in 1830 that devastated Meskwaki leadership. That year, a group of Dakota and Menominee attacked an unarmed delegation of Meskwaki leaders on their way to Prairie du Chien for a peace conference (Hagan 1958). All but one of the Meskwaki party were killed. The lone survivor was noted as being "half Winnebago" (Hagan 1958:117). While the record does not specify what line of Hochunk blood the survivor had, it does indicate the awareness of the mixed-blood status of that individual. A consequence of this massacre was a temporary void in Meskwaki leadership, which was filled by Mukwabwan 'Bear's Thigh', also known as Morgan. He was the son of a Scots-Irish man with the last name Morgan and is what the Meskwaki refer to as a 'blanket bred'. These were the children of non-native fathers, who were raised by the Meskwaki mothers, and they were in opposition to the 'civilized breeds', who were raised by their non-native fathers. Here we have an example of an individual who is Meskwaki not through the patrilineal line, but through the matrilineal line, ascending to the role of paramount tribal chief.

Surveys of more recent tribal rolls and census lists also yield interesting examples. In "The Meskwaki People of To-day," Ward (1906) includes a table of names that indicates non-Meskwaki parentage. Examples include the following:

1. Ash-e-tone-e-quot "George Morgan," listed as having a Potawatomi father and a Meskwaki mother (1906:195)
2. Na-na-que "said to be Sauki," with children listed on rolls with no reference to Sauk heritage, including Qua-squa-me, Albert Brown and Ma-ke-ta-ma-she-qua, Ed Brown (1906:198–199)
3. Ma-ma-sah "B[rother] of [number] 2 [George Morgan]," father of both listed as Potawatomi (1906:200)
4. Cha-ke-ma-co, Ma-ka-see-sa, and Na-wa-ta-na are listed as sons of female Wa-wa-co, who is listed as the wife of Jim Eagle who is "Sioux" (1906:202)
5. Ka-pa-who "Pottawotomi" (1906:207)
6. Ash-we-puc-ke-see "Sam Lincoln" Winnebago (1906:208)

7. Quin-e-pah "Sauki" (1906:209)
8. Wau-ke-mau-wit "Harry Davenport Sr." "son of Bailey Davenport" (1906:212) [Bailey Davenport is one of the two non-native sons of Col. Davenport]

There are twelve individuals on this one tribal list from the early 1900s that are listed as being either from another tribe, descended from a male from another tribe, or descended from a white male. It is common for these Meskwaki lists of this time period (pre-1937) to identify these types of individuals. What is also common is that mixed bloods from this time period will later be identified as full-blood Meskwaki (see below).

Why Patrilineal Descent?

The Meskwaki also have questions concerning the intent of the decision to make the patrilineal descent the only avenue for tribal membership. Discussions with a variety of Meskwaki across the factions and clans has led to five prevalent possible reasons for its inclusion in the Tribal Constitution: money issues, political factionalism, the insertion of the "adoption clause," the tribal leadership void, and the "great tribal membership reset."

The first issue is resources, primarily money and land. Of the five possible reasons for including the patrilineal membership requirement, this was the one most referred to by Meskwaki consultants. The primary resource concern was the issue of annuity payments. The annuity process, instituted through treaties, has been a long-standing issue among the Meskwaki. Issues with annuities arose from relationship predicaments with Indian agents, with traders, as well as with Meskwaki chiefs due to factionalism (Green 1974). Meskwaki discuss what were known as "Money Chiefs," individuals who were placed in leadership positions (chiefs) by the U.S. government simply because they could be paid to do what the government required, including limiting annuity payments to tribal members. Originally Meskwaki note that annuity payments were paid out to positions that were referred to as "head of household." In Meskwaki culture, heads of households could be either gender, male or female, but after the 1937 Tribal Constitution, only males were recognized as heads of household, which eliminated payments to female-headed households and increased payments to the male-headed households.

The secondary resource concern was land. While the Settlement land base was growing since the original purchase in 1857, the amount of usable land for farming was limited. By enforcing the patrilineal descent rule, the number of eligible tribal members (male-headed households) for the finite usable land was smaller (Zimmer 2016).

The second issue is political factionalism, which seems to predate the Fox Wars in the 1700s and has been viewed as an important corporate survival mechanism. Some Meskwaki suggest that at the time the tribal constitution was being developed, the progressive faction saw the opportunity to negatively impact the conservative faction by instituting the patrilineal membership rule in order to reduce the conservative faction's political base and overall enrolled numbers. The results of the constitutional vote were 80 votes in favor, 78 votes against. Today Meskwaki suggest that these numbers align with the two factions, and that the vote was simply split on factional lines.

The next issue concerns Section 10-5101 of the Tribal Constitution, otherwise known as the "adoption clause." This section stipulates that the tribal council can, by a simple majority vote, grant restricted (nonbenefits) tribal enrollment to anyone. Some Meskwaki refer to this as the "compromise clause," and speculate that it may have been inserted as a potential workaround to the patrilineal rule (Foley 1995). Since 1937, however, this clause has never been enacted.

After the adoption clause, the next issue discussed by Meskwaki in relation to the tribal membership requirement is the perceived tribal leadership void that followed the death of Chief Pushetonequa in 1919. Meskwaki observed that following the chief's death, the subsequent Indian agents filled the power vacuum with themselves, in some cases actually leading the existing council and later creating their own council (Green 1974). Some believe the decision to include the patrilineal requirement was made by the Indian agent, or some other government official, and that the decision reflects the western American cultural ideas of male dominance during that time period.

The last reason discussed by Meskwaki today concerning the inclusion of the patrilineal descent rule in the Tribal Constitution is what they refer to as the tribal roll reset. Meskwaki believe, and tribal rolls and other forms of official tribal information seem to support, the idea that at some point everyone on the tribal rolls, no matter the degree of Meskwaki blood, were "reset" to 100% Meskwaki. Allinson (1974) in "Education and the Mesquakie" discusses the Meskwaki in relation to the government boarding schools. In 1914 the Indian boarding schools adopted a policy requiring that a student be one quarter Indian blood for attendance at a boarding school (Allinson 1974). Allinson (1974:119) provided the blood quantum listing for the three Sac and Fox groups (Kansas Sauk, Oklahoma Sauk, and Iowa Meskwaki) for 1917 as follows:

> Iowa Meskwaki: Full blood 374—Over ½ blood 0—Under ½ blood 0
> Kansas Sauk: Full blood 0—Over ½ blood 12—Under ½ blood 84
> Oklahoma Sauk Kansas: Full blood 576—Over ½ blood 130—Under ½ blood 0

Allinson observed: "Listing all 374 of the settlement members as full bloods in 1927 is ridiculous as shown by documentary and empirical evidence" (1974:119). Allinson is correct, but this does illustrate the "reset" of blood quantum among the Meskwaki. Many Meskwaki feel that this reset allowed for the patrilineal descent rule to be included because it made everyone equal in terms of blood quantum and that the progressive leaders at the time did not foresee this becoming a divisive issue in the future. For example, one of the four-person progressive committee that drafted the tribal constitution was Ed Davenport. He was the son of Charlie Davenport, who was the son of Harry Davenport Sr., who was the son of Bailey Davenport, who was the son of Col. Davenport (Brown 1964:82). By the membership rule created by the constitution committee, this committee member, Ed Davenport, would not have been a tribal member.

These five possible reasons for including the patrilineal descent rule in the Tribal Constitution are still today points of tribal discussion. They are also tied to some degree to the consequences that have arisen since that vote in 1937.

Consequences of Patrilineal Descent

Following the incident on 8 May 2022, many simmering opinions boiled over privately and publicly. Fieldwork during 2022 and 2023 yielded six main discussion topics relating to the membership rule, what many Meskwaki feel are either contemporary consequences of the 1937 vote or recent adjustments made to deal with the rule. These topics are (1) resources, (2) the male "honor code," (3) continued factionalism, (4) the influence of the outside world, and (5) the rise of the "cultural Meskwaki."

With the addition of the tribal casino and other business ventures in recent years the Meskwaki tribal economic situation has grown and allowed for further economic ventures as well as the continuance of, and an increase in, per capita payments and benefits to tribal members. If the tribe were to change the membership rule and therefore allow those who were descended from Meskwaki mothers to receive benefits, the amount of the per capita payments, housing, and land assignments as well as other tribal benefits would decrease. Tribal resource concerns continue to be at the forefront of Meskwaki life (Foley 1995).

Historically, a Meskwaki father had the responsibility to enroll his children with the tribe through an "acknowledgement of paternity" affidavit if the parents were not married. This was referred to as the "honor code" in terms of enrollment purposes. In fact, the honor code extended beyond just the biological father. During fieldwork, examples were discovered from the last 50 years where men claimed children that were not biologically theirs (some were brothers of the biological father, or other male relatives). But over the last 20 years, enough men have been refusing to enroll their children that amendments to the Tribal Constitution were passed during the period of 2007–17 that introduced a woman's ability through a DNA test to enroll a child. Today people note that the "honor code" has been replaced by a "deadbeat dad code."

The next perceived consequence of the patrilineal descent rule is the continuance of the progressive/conservative factionalism. This factionalism from the early 1900s has been continued through the present by their descendants and in many ways has also become a full blood/mixed blood issue. As time passes the number of mixed bloods has increased, and intermarriage has grown within the Meskwaki community. Many Meskwaki believe that the full-blood members are attempting to maintain their power by withholding tribal membership from those mixed bloods from non-Meskwaki fathers.

The fifth perceived consequence is the belief that the outside world is influencing Meskwaki culture. Females in larger numbers have left the Settlement over the last 90 years for a variety of reasons, such as for education purposes, initially boarding schools and nontribal K–12 schools, but now for undergraduate and graduate educations. Other factors such as increased travel, economic growth, as well as participation in Indigenous events including powwows, have provided Meskwaki women the opportunity to enter into relationships that resulted in children with non-Meskwaki males. It is believed that the draw of the outside world, and of outside males, is strong, with many believing that the lack of support in the current Meskwaki community is driving females away.

The sixth and final contemporary issue, the rise of the "cultural Meskwaki," became the focus of our research following the events of 8 May 2022. In a sense, all the previous historic and contemporary issues are interwoven together into this issue. As a category, cultural Meskwaki are non-enrollment-eligible individuals (males or females) who are recognized by those that practice Meskwaki culture, either through religion or social activities, as being participating members of Meskwaki society. For many, participation is the key to being Meskwaki, not the amount of Meskwaki blood or which side of the family is Meskwaki. Action, what you do, is viewed by many as more important than whether or not you are enrolled. There have always been "cultural Meskwaki," from even before the 1937 Tribal Constitution. Consultants today will remark that historically their numbers were all very low, in comparison to the growing number today. In addition, consultants will point out that currently "cultural Meskwaki" are now filling key religious and cultural roles across the community, yet they receive no benefits from the tribe. Many are perplexed how those they rely on for cultural and religious guidance are not assisted in any way.

At the end of 2023, several cultural Meskwaki, including an individual of religious importance, were removed from tribal housing. The Tribal Constitution distinguishes between two basic types of land assignments: the first is agricultural land that may also contain a homesite, and the second is just a homesite. Both types of land assignments may be inherited and willed to members of the tribe upon the death of the previous assignee. The issue at the end of 2023 occurred because the previous assignee is the last enrolled member of the family, and upon their death the other individuals who were residing in the house have no legal claim to remain. In December 2023 multiple land assignments were reclaimed by the tribe, and nonenrolled individuals and families were evicted. During this process attempts were made to find solutions—options such as the "adoption clause" were proposed and denied, extensions were granted—but in the end the determination was eviction.

Conclusion

Since the establishment of the patrilineal descent rule for Meskwaki tribal membership in 1937 there have been individuals who have been negatively affected by that decision. As the nonenrolled numbers grow over the years, their impacts affect more and more Meskwaki. For many, but not yet a majority, the 1937 membership rule is a product of the U.S. government or outside non-Meskwaki traditions, not a tribal tradition. Frustrations are being voiced, with modifications made to appease those affected in recent years, such as the amendment to the Tribal Constitution to allow women to enroll their children with the aid of a DNA test. Some express their displeasure at tribal gatherings or on social media, while some will go as far as to vandalize tribal property to have their opinion known. At some point in the future, the majority of tribal members may be in favor of changing the membership requirement in the Tribal Constitution, or perhaps a tribal council will see fit to make the change. In fact, their sister group, the Sauk of Oklahoma, have over time amended their Tribal Constitution's membership requirement, reducing it now to requiring only one quarter Sauk blood from either side of the family.

Since their creation out of bloody earth, the Meskwaki have sought a way of life that ensured their survival. Gendered individuals and groups have worked equally together to accomplish the required tasks to ensure the continuance of the Meskwaki and their world. Throughout their history as Meskwaki, survival has been their guiding principle, and at some point in the future they will be forced to make a decision in regard to their membership rule. To ensure their survival, the decision seems obvious to many, but to the current majority, it is not time yet. But for a growing number of Meskwaki, the question remains, "How can you be proud to be Meskwaki if half the tribe doesn't matter to you?"

NOTES

1. Fieldwork for this paper was undertaken by the authors on the Meskwaki Settlement from spring 2022 through fall 2023. Fieldwork was sought with members of all the active clans and across factional lines, attempting to acquire a balanced portrayal of Meskwaki points of view concerning this subject matter. Considering the delicacy of this subject, all consultants are anonymous, and all references to current opinions are from our recent fieldwork. Meskwaki terms follow Goddard and Thomason (2014).
2. For general overviews of Meskwaki factionalism, see Gearing (1970) and Foley (1995).
3. There is debate in the Meskwaki community concerning who actually included the patrilineal descent rule in the Tribal Constitution, either the four-person committee or the Indian agent (Foley 1995); regardless of the source, the rule was included.

4. The Meskwaki also practiced the levirate, the corresponding practice of replacing a dead husband in a marriage with a male relative, typically a brother or male cousin.

REFERENCES

Allinson, MacBurnie. 1974. Education and the Mesquakie. PhD thesis, Iowa State University.

Brown, Richard Frank. 1964. A Social History of the Mesquakie Indians, 1800–1963. MS thesis, Iowa State University.

Callender, Charles. 1962. *Social Organization of the Central Algonkian Indians*. Publications in Anthropology 7. Milwaukee: Milwaukee Public Museum.

Callender, Charles. 1978a. Great Lakes-Riverine Sociopolitical Organization. *Handbook of North American Indians*, vol, 15: *Northeast*, ed. by Bruce Trigger, pp. 610–621. Washington, DC: Smithsonian Institution.

Callender, Charles. 1978b. Fox. *Handbook of North American Indians*, vol. 15: *Northeast*, ed. by Bruce Trigger, pp. 636–647. Washington, DC: Smithsonian Institution.

Callender, Charles. 1994. Central Algonkian Moieties. *North American Indian Anthropology Essays in Society and Culture*, ed. by Raymond J. DeMallie and Alfonso Ortiz, pp. 108–124. Norman: University of Oklahoma Press.

Eggan, Fred. 1955. Social Anthropology: Methods and Results. *Social Anthropology of North American Tribes*, ed. by Fred Eggan, pp. 485–554. Chicago: University of Chicago Press.

Foley, Douglas E. 1995. *The Heartland Chronicles*. Philadelphia: University of Pennsylvania Press.

Forsyth, Thomas. 1912. An Account of the Manners and Customs of the Sauk and Fox Nations of Indian Traditions. *The Indian Tribes of the Upper Mississippi Valley and Region of the Great Lakes*, ed. by Emma H. Blair, 2:183–245. Cleveland: Arthur H. Clark.

Gearing, Frederick O. 1970. *The Face of the Fox*. Chicago: Aldine.

Goddard, Ives. 1975. Fox Social Organization 1650–1850. *Papers of the Sixth Algonquian Conference*, ed. by William Cowan, pp. 128–140. National Museum of Man, Mercury Series, Canadian Ethnology Service Papers 23. Ottawa: National Museums of Canada.

Goddard, Ives, and Lucy Thomason. 2014. *A Meskwaki–English and English–Meskwaki Dictionary, Based on Early Twentieth-Century Writings by Native Speakers*. Petoskey, MI: Mundart Press.

Green, Michael D. 1974. The Sac-Fox Annuity Crisis of 1840 in Iowa Territory. *Arizona and the West* 16(2):141–156.

Hagan, William T. 1958. *The Sac and Fox Indians*. Norman: University of Oklahoma Press.

Jones, William. 1939. *Ethnography of the Fox Indians*, ed. by Margaret Fischer. Bureau of

American Ethnology Bulletin 125. Washington, DC: Smithsonian Institution.

Marston, Morrell. 1912. Letter to Reverend Dr. Jedidiah Morse, by Major Morrell Marsten, U.S.A., Commanding at Fort Armstrong, Ill., November, 1820. *The Indian Tribes of the Upper Mississippi Valley and Region of the Great Lakes*, ed. by Emma H. Blair, 2:139–182. Cleveland: Arthur H. Clark.

Meskwaki Nation. 1937. Tribal Constitution, Codes & Bylaws. https://www.meskwaki.org/constitution/.

Michelson, Truman. 1925. The Autobiography of a Fox Woman. *Annual Report of the Bureau of American Ethnology for the Years 1918–1919*, 40:291–349. Washington, DC: G. P. O.

Morgan, Lewis H. 1964 [1877]. *Ancient Society*. Cambridge, MA: Harvard University Press.

Perrot, Nicolas. 1911. Memoir on the Manners, Customs, and Religion of the Savages of North America. *The Indian Tribes of the Upper Mississippi Valley and Region of the Great Lakes*, ed. by Emma H. Blair, 1:23–272. Cleveland: Arthur H. Clark.

Tax, Sol. 1955. The Social Organization of the Fox Indians. *Social Anthropology of North American Tribes*, ed. by Fred Eggan, pp. 243–282. Chicago: University of Chicago Press.

Thwaites, Reuben Gold. 1896–1901. *The Jesuit Relations and Allied Documents*. 73 vols. Cleveland: Burrows Brothers.

Ward, Duren. 1906. The Meskwaki People of To-day. *Iowa Journal of History and Politics* 4(2):190–219.

Zimmer, Eric. 2016. Red Earth Nation: Environment and Sovereignty in Modern Meskwaki History. PhD thesis, University of Iowa.

Le Pluriel Nominal Préfixé d'un Parler Cri

Stéphane Goyette

Le but de cet article est de démontrer l'existence, dans un parler cri, de morphèmes marquant le pluriel qui ont la particularité de provenir du français.[1] Plus précisément, nous examinerons de plus près les pluriels de certains noms d'origine française dans le parler cri de l'Île-à-la Crosse (CIALC). Le fort de l'Île-à-la-Crosse, situé dans ce qui est aujourd'hui le nord de la province canadienne de la Saskatchewan, fut fondé (comme poste de traite) en 1776 (Marsh 2015). De ce fait, il a dû constituer une des premières zones de contact entre les Français et les Premières Nations des Prairies canadiennes. Aussi ne doit-on nullement s'étonner d'y trouver aujourd'hui un parler cri très francisé du point de vue lexical.

Comme dans tous les parlers cris et dans toutes les langues algonquiennes, les noms d'origine autochtone (algonquienne) forment leur pluriel au moyen de suffixes qui diffèrent selon le genre grammatical (animé/inanimé) du nom. Ce système de marquage des noms au pluriel remonte au proto-algonquien et demeure vivant dans toutes les langues de la famille algonquienne (autrement dit, dans toutes les langues qui continuent le proto-algonquien), y compris tous les parlers cris.

La particularité du CIALC est qu'on y trouve aussi une minorité de noms, d'origine française, dont le pluriel se forme au moyen de ce qui (à première vue) semble être des préfixes remontant étymologiquement aux articles définis français. La question sera de savoir si l'on peut ou non, en synchronie, voir en ces éléments de véritables préfixes en CIALC. L'autre possibilité serait que ces noms à pluriel préfixé seraient des pluriels irréguliers en CIALC, sans que les locuteurs ne perçoivent le préfixe comme constituant un morphème distinct.

Histoire de la Recherche

Bakker (1997) a été le premier à signaler l'existence du CIALC en tant que variété de cri qui, tout en ayant emprunté un nombre élevé de mots français, était et demeure bien distincte (tant sur les plans synchronique que diachronique) du mitchif.[2] Ces mots d'origine française en CIALC sont pour la plupart inconnus des autres parlers cris voisins (données tirées de Ahenakew 2009):

(1) a. lilit 'lit'
  b. l'batô 'traversier' (ferry)
  c. lames 'messe'
  d. lashâmp 'chambre à coucher' (bedroom)
  e. lîpwâ '(les) pois'

À première vue, il n'y a ici rien de bien étonnant: les noms ont été empruntés avec leur article défini, aboutissant à *l* ou *li* pour les noms masculins singuliers, *la* pour les féminins singuliers et *lî* pour les pluriels.

En synchronie, bien entendu, rien ne justifie que l'on voie en ces éléments des articles: comme les mots français issus de l'arabe avec un *al* initial provenant de l'article défini arabe (alcool, algorithme . . .), cet élément pourrait sembler sans pertinence grammaticale en CIALC.

Cependant, les apparences sont trompeuses: examinons les noms suivants:

(2) a. l'kotô 'couteau' / lîkotô 'couteaux'
  b. lakilot 'culotte' / lîkilot 'culottes' (Jeans)
  c. l'biskwî 'biscuit' / lîbiskwî 'biscuits'

On voit que ces noms n'ont pas seulement été empruntés au français, mais que, du point de vue morphologique, ils opposent un singulier et un pluriel d'origine française (issus tous les deux de l'article défini français et de ses formes distinctes au singulier et au pluriel, en fait).

Ceci n'est pas vrai de tous les noms empruntés au français en CIALC. Les données du vocabulaire CIALC permettent d'ailleurs de se faire une certaine idée de différentes strates de vocabulaire français, aboutissant parfois à d'intéressants doublets. Qu'on compare *l'patak/lîpatak* 'SING-patate / PLUR-patate' désignant (au singulier et au pluriel) la 'patate', et *napatak/napataķwa*, 'patate-SING / patate-PLUR', avec le même sens et un suffixe du pluriel purement cri. Ce dernier mot indique qu'une première vague de mots français a dû être absorbée par le CIALC ancien sans modification de l'inventaire de phonèmes (d'où le remplacement du /l/ français par /n/) ni emprunt de morphème lié (au contraire, on voit que l'emprunt a subi une intégration morphologique qui détonne par rapport au sort qu'a subi la strate ultérieure de mots français ayant donné naissance aux préfixes de nombre nominal).

On se doit de souligner que, même si ces préfixes ne se retrouvent qu'avec certains noms d'origine française en CIALC, il s'agit déjà là d'une situation remarquable et qui paraît tout à fait unique, non seulement parmi les langues algonquiennes ayant emprunté des noms au français, mais encore parmi n'importe quelle langue autochtone des Amériques ayant emprunté des noms au français.

Ce fait est doublement remarquable si l'on se souvient que l'anglais, et non le français, constitue (aujourd'hui!) la langue seconde des locuteurs natifs du CIALC. Or, un cas clair d'influence française de ce type (avec emprunt de noms singuliers et pluriels distincts qui maintiennent la distinction de nombre) paraît tout à fait inconnu même dans le cas de langues autochtones des Amériques (algonquiennes ou non) dont les locuteurs ont toujours le français comme langue seconde. Bakker et Papen (2008:253) l'affirment très clairement.

Ainsi, en innu, selon Drapeau (1980), on observe bel et bien (dans le cas des emprunts plus récents seulement) l'utilisation productive d'un morphème /le/, issu de l'article défini pluriel français (*les*), préfixé aux noms empruntés au français et marquant ainsi leur statut d'emprunts. Cette adaptation se fait sans toutefois conférer au nom emprunté une valeur plurielle. Pour marquer le nombre nominal, la morphologie de l'innu demeure la seule possibilité.

La question qui se pose à propos des noms à marque "préfixée" de nombre du CIALC (tels que ceux donnés ci-dessus) est la suivante: peut-on parler en synchronie de préfixes de nombre nominal en CIALC, ou devrait-on plutôt voir ces noms d'origine française comme étant de simples pluriels irréguliers (lexicalisés)? Dans ce dernier cas, ces "préfixes" seraient comparables aux désinences de pluriels latins ou grecs que l'on retrouve par exemple en anglais (*stadium/stadia, stigma/stigmata*), qui ont été empruntés tels quels et dont les désinences (de singulier ou de pluriel) ne manifestent strictement aucune réelle productivité en anglais moderne.

Vu le fait qu'en innu, malgré l'omniprésence du français, il n'existe aucune trace de préfixes d'origine française marquant le nombre, il pourrait sembler plus prudent de prendre la seconde hypothèse (pluriels irréguliers lexicalisés) comme point de départ plutôt que la première. Mais à en juger du titre de cet article, on pourrait soupçonner (avec raison) qu'on penche vers la première solution. C'est-à dire que les éléments marquant le pluriel dans des paires telles que *l'kotô* 'couteau' / *lîkotô* 'couteaux' constituent réellement, en synchronie, des préfixes marqueurs de nombre nominal.

Dans ce qui suit, nous expliquerons pourquoi nous croyons qu'il est préférable de parler, en CIALC, d'un préfixe *lî-* marquant les pluriels nominaux dont le singulier commence par *l-* ou *la-*.

Le Préfixe (?) de Nombre

Voici quelques autres paires singuliers/pluriels de noms d'origine française en CIALC:

(3) a. l'miten/lîmiten 'mitaine(s)'
    b. l'krrep /lîkrrep 'crêpe(s)'
    c. l'pinås/lîpinås 'punaise(s)'

Ce que paraissent indiquer ces données est une généralisation du "préfixe" *l-* aux dépens du "préfixe" *la-*. En effet, on ne trouve aucun exemple de *la-* à la place d'un *l-* justifié par l'étymologie. Cela est encourageant pour qui désirerait défendre la thèse selon laquelle on aurait affaire ici à des préfixes: comme le montrent bien les exemples ci-dessus, tant la forme de l'article masculin singulier devant une consonne que la forme du singulier (masculin et féminin) devant une voyelle aboutit à /l / en CIALC. Si, après avoir emprunté ces noms avec leurs articles définis, les locuteurs ont perçu /l/ et /la/ comme deux simples allomorphes (à la distribution lexicalisée) d'un préfixe singulier s'opposant au préfixe du pluriel, /li/, il n'y aurait rien d'étonnant à ce que l'allomorphe le plus fréquent, /l/, connaisse une extension aux dépens du moins fréquent, /la/.

Les données suivantes sont encore plus claires.

(4) a. l'zayöň/ lîzayöň 'oignon(s)'
b. l'zarrâňsh/ lîzarrâňsh 'orange(s)'
c. l'zigwi/lîzigwi 'aiguille(s)'

On voit ici qu'on ne peut considérer ces pluriels CIALC comme de simples lexicalisations de mots d'emprunt français: il est certain qu'en français parlé à l'époque de ces emprunts (18ème/19ème siècle), les singuliers devaient être sensiblement les mêmes qu'en français moderne: *l'oignon, l'orange, l'aiguille.* On voit que les formes du pluriel en CIALC proviennent tout droit des formes françaises *les oignons, les oranges, les aiguilles*, avec réalisation du /z/ de liaison.[3]

De l'Origine de Certains Pluriels du CIALC

Si l'on accepte que *lî-* constitue un préfixe de pluriel nominal en CIALC, cependant, les formes CIALC modernes s'expliquent aisément: il faudrait supposer deux étapes:

Étape I: En CIALC ancien, il faut supposer que les emprunts ci-dessous avaient les formes suivantes:

(5) a. *l'ayöň/ lîzayöň 'oignon(s)'
b. *l'arrâňsh/ lîzarrâňsh 'orange(s)'
c. *l'igwi/lîzigwi 'aiguille(s)'

-et qu'ils coexistaient avec d'autres emprunts, tel que ceux vus ci-dessous:

(2) a. l'kotô 'couteau' / lîkotô 'couteaux'
b. lakilot 'culotte' / lîkilot 'culottes'(jeans)
c. l'biskwî 'biscuit' / lîbiskwî 'biscuits'

On se doit de souligner que cette coexistence postulée n'a aucun lien ni avec la chronologie relative des différents emprunts, ni avec celle de la chronologie possible de l'emprunt, à différentes époques, de noms singuliers et pluriels entrés séparément en CIALC.

Étape II: Ré-analyse et régularisation.

Si on suppose que *lî-* était bel et bien un préfixe de pluriel nominal en CIALC, alors le passage de

(6) a. *l'ayöň
b. *l'arrâňsh
c. *l'igwi

aux nouvelles formes (attestées) en CIALC,

(7) a. l'zayöň
b. l'zarrâňsh
c. l'zigwi

serait un cas de régularisation analogique fort banal, suivant le modèle des autres pluriels issus du français: si les pluriels à préfixe du type *l'biskwî* 'biscuit' *lîbiskwî* 'biscuits' étaient les plus fréquents, il n'y aurait rien d'étonnant à ce que l'on ait refait les anciens singuliers en partant du pluriel moins le préfixe *lî-* du pluriel et avec ajout du préfixe *l-* du singulier.

Mais cette réanalyse présuppose que les locuteurs du CIALC devaient percevoir *lî-* comme un morphème lié au nom marquant le pluriel.[4]

Quelques Conclusions

1. Le CIALC est unique non seulement comme parler cri, mais encore comme langue algonquienne: à notre connaissance, il n'existe AUCUNE langue (ni dialecte particulier d'une langue) de la famille algonquienne autre que le CIALC faisant usage de préfixes de pluriel pour certains noms.

2. Plus remarquable encore, il n'existe à notre connaissance aucun autre cas d'une langue formant ses pluriels nominaux avec des suffixes ayant emprunté de préfixe nominal formant le pluriel (ayant emprunté d'élément qui synchroniquement est perçu par les locuteurs de la langue emprunteuse comme étant un préfixe marquant le pluriel, pour être plus précis). Le CIALC est donc remarquable comme produit de contact langagier (franco-cri), le mitchif ayant peut-être trop attiré d'attention sur ce point.

Quelques Conséquences de Ce Qui Précède

Si l'on accepte le raisonnement présenté ci-dessus, il en découle un certain nombre de conséquences très intéressantes portant sur l'histoire comme sur la nature des contacts langagiers entre Français et membres des Premières Nations à l'époque coloniale.

En effet, une question qui a longtemps préoccupé les chercheurs s'intéressant à la diffusion de vocables français (et plus largement européens) dans les langues des Premières Nations est celle de la source directe ou indirecte de ces emprunts: si l'on retrouve un mot d'origine française dans plus qu'une langue des Premières Nations, cela signifie-t-il que les deux langues auraient chacune emprunté le mot au français, ou alors que le mot constituerait un emprunt (d'origine française) qui serait passé d'une langue amérindienne à une autre, sans que le français ne joue directement de rôle?

Or, plusieurs chercheurs se servent de la morphologie du mot comme critère servant à séparer les mots d'origine française passés directement dans une langue amérindienne de ceux passés d'une langue amérindienne à l'autre. Dremeaux (2004:20), par exemple, qui étudie les mots d'origine française dans les langues athabascanes septentrionales, constate que le mot désignant la *caisse* dans ces langues paraît provenir pour certaines langues du singulier français (*la caisse*) et pour d'autres du pluriel français (*les caisses*): elle en conclut que ce mot doit provenir, dans ces langues, d'un contact direct avec le français.

Si on accepte la thèse de cet article, cependant, on voit bien que cette conclusion doit être mise en doute. En effet, on pourrait supposer que le mot aurait existé en CIALC[5] avec alternance **la-/lî-* au singulier et au pluriel, et que différentes langues athabascanes auraient tout bonnement chacune choisi de généraliser une seule de ces deux formes. Dans l'état actuel de nos connaissances, nous ne savons pas et ne pouvons pas non plus savoir d'ailleurs si le mot en question (et d'autres mots montrant le même type de variation dans les langues athabascanes septentrionales) proviendrait directement du français ou d'un stade ancien du CIALC qui aurait possédé ce mot.[6]

Quelques Questions sur Lesquelles Devront se Pencher les Chercheurs à l'Avenir

Tout d'abord, une question qui mériterait une étude plus approfondie que ce que nous pouvons effectuer dans cet article porterait sur l'origine des préfixes en CIALC:

leur source est française, cela ne fait aucun doute, mais comment se fait-il qu'on ne retrouve aucun emprunt morphologique de ce type nulle part ailleurs dans l'ensemble du domaine algonquien? Ni même, plus largement, dans l'ensemble des langues des Premières Nations?

La question est d'autant plus pertinente que l'innu, qui pourtant diffère du CIALC du fait de ne former ses pluriels nominaux qu'avec des morphèmes autochtones, fait un usage productif d'un préfixe issu d'un article défini français emprunté, /le/.[7]

Encore plus remarquable est le fait que l'on retrouve, dans une communauté de langue innue (celle de Betsiamites), une francisation de la langue des jeunes générations aboutissant à une langue mixte (aux noms français et au verbe innu) qui ressemble singulièrement au mitchif (Voir Bakker 1997:184-186, qui examine tant les ressemblances que les différences). Bien que l'on qualifie souvent le mitchif de langue unique (le "nec plus ultra" des grammaires en contact, pour reprendre le titre de Papen 1987), le CIALC semblerait, avec ses préfixes de nombre nominal issus d'articles définis français, mériter tout autant ce titre, dans la mesure où aucune langue autochtone d'Amérique du Nord (algonquienne ou non) ne semble avoir effectué semblable emprunt.

La question se pose donc: pourquoi? Pourquoi le contact entre le français et le cri, dont la progéniture actuelle est (*inter alia*) le CIALC, a-t-il ainsi donné naissance à une forme de cri aussi unique sur le plan typologique?

Il est difficile de ne pas se demander si la réponse à cette question aurait un rapport avec le fait curieux, que signale Dremeaux (2004:22), que dans les emprunts français dans les langues athabascanes septentrionales on trouve certains noms sans article défini et une majorité de noms avec article défini agglutiné, mais qu'on ne trouve aucun nom avec agglutination d'un article partitif ou indéfini.[8] Bakker et Papen (2008:261) signalent la même particularité (présence ou absence d'article défini, mais absence catégorique de tout autre article) dans les emprunts français en carrier.[9] On notera qu'il ne s'agit aucunement d'une loi universelle: Drapeau (1980:31-33) signale de nombreux mots d'emprunts français en innu avec un article indéfini pluriel (/te:ba:dew/ 'pâté', dont l'étymon est 'des pâtés').

En effet, si, pour une raison quelconque, l'article défini s'est vu privilégié comme forme liée à l'emprunt nominal français en CIALC ancien, il est bien possible que cette fréquence supérieure (comparée à des langues amérindiennes dont les emprunts français auraient contenu une plus forte proportion de noms sans article défini agglutiné) de noms avec /l/, /la/, au singulier et /lî/ au pluriel aurait contribué à ce que les locuteurs en arrivent à percevoir ces éléments comme d'authentiques préfixes marqueurs de nombre.

Un second point qui mérite d'être examiné avec soin porte sur la phonologie du CIALC, et plus particulièrement celle de son élément français. En effet, les entrées et l'introduction du dictionnaire d'Ahenakew semblent indiquer que plusieurs phonèmes français semblent s'être conservés dans les emprunts français du CIALC. Ainsi, un doublet en CIALC tel que *lirribâň/sirapân*, 'rubans' (le premier ayant comme étymon 'les rubans', le second 'ses rubans', à en croire Brown 1999:125), où la graphie de la dernière syllabe du premier mot paraît bien indiquer une voyelle nasale (et non une voyelle suivie d'un /n /, comme dans la dernière syllabe du second mot) laisse croire que le second mot serait le plus ancien en raison de sa moindre adaptation phonologique au système cri. Qu'on compare le cas du doublet désignant la patate, présenté ci-dessus. C'est donc dire que le CIALC a sans doute joué un rôle dans la diffusion dans l'Ouest canadien du mot provenant de 'ses rubans', avec tout le respect dû à l'avis contraire de Bakker et Papen (2008:266).

Ce fait a toute son importance: on l'a mentionné ci-dessus, l'analyse morphologique que nous venons de présenter remet en cause bien des conclusions sur la source la plus immédiate (française ou autochtone) de mots d'emprunts français en Amérique du Nord, vu que des mots à étymon français provenant du CIALC (du singulier ou du pluriel) pourraient bien donner l'illusion de provenir du français même. Or, si le CIALC a également conservé dans ses emprunts des phonèmes français inconnus de toute autre forme de cri, tout recours à des critères phonologiques afin de distinguer les emprunts directs des emprunts indirects risque de s'avérer tout aussi fragile. Encore une fois, on doit remettre en question toute une série de conclusions et les réexaminer si l'on veut se faire une idée juste des rôles du français d'une part et de diverses langues amérindiennes (notamment diverses *lingua franca* amérindiennes, comme le soutient Brown 1999) de l'autre en ce qui concerne l'histoire de la diffusion de différents noms d'origine française en Amérique du Nord.

Enfin, ceci soulève une dernière question qui mériterait l'attention de chercheurs en linguistique algonquienne: dans quelle mesure - vu l'abondance de mots d'emprunts français, la productivité du préfixe nominal marquant le nombre tiré des formes de l'article défini français, le nombre de phonèmes français étrangers au cri toujours présents dans divers emprunts- le français aurait-il influencé d'autres aspects (sémantique, morphosyntaxe) du CIALC? Cette question est indissociable, selon nous, d'une autre beaucoup plus large: au-delà du lexique, quel a été l'impact du français sur l'ensemble des parlers cris, particulièrement ceux utilisés dans les Prairies?

Conclusion

Dans cet article, nous avons cherché à démontrer - au moyen d'une analyse de changements diachroniques - que les noms d'origine française en CIALC avec /l/ ou /la/ au singulier et /lî / au pluriel sont bel et bien pourvus d'un morphème préfixé marquant le nombre (et non la définitude, le genre et le nombre, comme en français), et ne sont pas des noms d'emprunt à la morphologie improductive en cri.

Nous en avons conclu que la présence de ce système en CIALC rend douteuse les tentatives faites par divers chercheurs de distinguer l'emprunt direct et l'emprunt indirect en se servant du critère morphologique (la variation entre article défini singulier et pluriel). Nous avons mentionné que la présence en CIALC de phonèmes français et non cris dans ces mêmes emprunts rend tout aussi douteuse une distinction entre emprunt direct et emprunt indirect au moyen de critères phonologiques.

Enfin, nous avons examiné ce qui reste à effectuer comme recherches sur le CIALC, son histoire et son interaction avec diverses langues, dont le français.

NOTES

1. Je désire remercier les participants du cinquante-cinquième colloque du Congrès des Algonquinistes (2023) présents lors de la présentation qui a servi de base à cet article, ainsi que deux lecteurs anonymes: leurs questions et commentaires en ont amélioré le fond comme la forme. Je les remercie tous, tout en soulignant que *Ubi peccavi, ego solus scripsi.*
2. Dans cet article on qualifiera de *mitchif* la langue mixte (essentiellement constituée de verbes cris et de noms et adjectifs français) parlée par une minorité de descendants des Métis de la colonie de la rivière Rouge. Il importe que le lecteur comprenne que le terme *mitchif*, parmi les Métis eux-mêmes, peut servir de façon plus large à désigner toute forme de français ou de cri ou d'autres langues parlées par des Métis de l'Ouest canadien (le titre de l'ouvrage de Ahenakew -voir la bibliographie-ne doit pas induire en erreur: il s'agit bel et bien d'un dictionnaire du cri de l'Île-à-la-Crosse, qui, étant parlé par des Métis, est qualifié de *mitchif*).
3. Pour les lecteurs dont la connaissance du français se limite à la forme écrite, il faut

préciser que l'article défini pluriel « les » a une réalisation /lɛ, le/ devant consonne et /lɛz, lez/ -dont le /z/ est dit "de liaison" -devant une voyelle. Ceci est tout aussi vrai du français normatif moderne que du français parlé par les voyageurs et explorateurs à l'époque coloniale.

4. On ne peut, de ce qui précède, conclure que les locuteurs ACTUELS du CIALC perçoivent *lî-* comme préfixe marquant le pluriel de certains noms. Cependant, on ne peut que conclure que les locuteurs du CIALC devaient percevoir que *lî-* était un préfixe marquant le pluriel de certains noms AU MOMENT OÙ LE CHANGEMENT ANALOGIQUE PRÉSENTÉ CI-DESSUS A EU LIEU.
5. Nous renvoyons à notre premier paragraphe: le fort de l'Île-à-la-Crosse a été fondé à une date très ancienne et a donc dû constituer un des premiers, sinon le premier point de contact stable entre Français et membres des Premières Nations à l'époque coloniale, et de ce fait il n'y a rien d'absurde à supposer que le cri qui s'y parlait aurait véhiculé des mots d'origine française qui se retrouvent dans d'autres langues amérindiennes de la région.
6. On ne trouve aucun mot dans le dictionnaire d'Ahenakew (2009) remontant à (*la*) *caisse*, mais rien n'exclut qu'un tel mot aurait déjà existé en CIALC.
7. Voir la présentation de la situation en innu dans la seconde section de cet article. Il pourrait s'agir d'un trait partagé avec d'autres langues autochtones d'Amérique du Nord: Dremeaux (2004, pages 18-20) n'examine pas dans quelle mesure le «"morphème" lV- issu de *le/le/les* aurait joui de productivité en tant que marque d'emprunt, comme en innu.
8. L'autrice parle d'article partitif seulement, mais comme le montrent ses exemples, on ne trouve aucun exemple clair d'article indéfini agglutiné non plus.
9. Il serait bon de signaler que la thèse de Prunet (1990), selon laquelle le carrier doit avoir emprunté directement ses noms au français, semble bien douteuse aux yeux de l'auteur de ces lignes, qui souhaite se pencher plus en détail sur la question lors de recherches ultérieures.

BIBLIOGRAPHIE

Ahenakew, Vince. 2009. *Nêhiyawêwin Masinahikan = Michif*/Cree Dictionary*. Saskatoon: Gabriel Dumont Institute.

Bakker, Peter. 1997. *A Language of Our Own: The Genesis of Michif, the Mixed Cree-French Language of the Canadian Métis*. Oxford: Oxford University Press.

Bakker, Peter, et Robert Papen. 2008. French influence on the native languages of Canada and adjacent USA. *Aspects of Language Contact: New Theoretical, Methodological and Empirical Findings with Special Focus on Romancisation Processes*, ed. by Thomas Stolz, Dirk Bakker and Rose Salas Palomo, pp. 239–286. Berlin: Mouton De Gruyter.

Brown, Cecil. 1999. *Lexical Acculturation in Native American Languages*. New York: Oxford University Press.

Drapeau, Lynn. 1980. Les Emprunts au Français en Montagnais. *Cahier de linguistique* 10: 29–49.

Dremeaux, Lillie. 2004. Slavey Jargon and the presence of French loanwords in Northern Athabaskan. Senior thesis, Swarthmore college.

Marsh, James. 2015 [2012]. L'Île-à-la-Crosse. *L'Encyclopédie canadienne*. https://www.thecanadianencyclopedia.ca/fr/article/ile-a-la-crosse.

Papen, Robert. 1987. Le Métif: Le Nec Plus Ultra des Grammaires en Contact. *Revue Québécoise de Linguistique Théorique et Appliquée* 6(2): 57–70.

Prunet, Jean-François. 1990. The Origin and Interpretation of French Loans in Carrier. *International journal of American Linguistics* 56(4): 484–502.

Preverb Order in Potawatomi

Robert E. Lewis Jr.

This paper provides an analysis of preverb order in Potawatomi.[1] I show that the ordering is not always entirely consistent and develop an analysis along the lines of Dahlstrom (1995) in terms of preverb topicalization. Previous research has argued that the order of preverbs in Menominee (Cook 2003) and Oji-Cree (Slavin 2005) can be accounted for via semantic classes.[2] This paper ultimately proposes a semantic class order of preverbs based on an analysis of a text corpus (Hockett 1937, 1940a,b,c).

The paper first provides necessary background information. It introduces the Potawatomi verb, reviews Hockett's (1948) comments on the ordering of preverbs in Potawatomi, and catalogs the inventory of preverbs.

The paper next investigates an overall ordering of preverbs via a corpus analysis. I describe the methodology used, outline the corpus, and present the findings. I found 82 types of combinations of two or more preverbs. I then ran a simple sorting algorithm on the observed combinations in an attempt to determine their overall relative order. This sort does not converge on a single overall ordering, as there are contradictory orders of preverbs found. A potential solution is suggested: to analyze one of the preverbs in these orderings as a topicalized preverb following Dahlstrom 1995.

The paper then provides an analysis of the data using the following four ordered semantic classes:[3]

(1) MODAL > ASPECT > SPATIAL > ADVERB

Background

The Potawatomi Verb Complex

The verb complex in Potawatomi, as in other Algonquian languages, is maximally composed of a stem, one or more preverbs, and inflectional morphology before and/or after the preverb and stem. As in other Algonquian languages, basic Potawatomi verb stems are maximally tripartite (Bloomfield 1962; Goddard 1975, 1990), containing an initial, medial, and final. Preverbs can be added to the beginning of a verb stem in order to modify it. They can encode lexical or functional information such as adverbial modification, tense, aspect, modality, and elements often translated into English with control predicates (e.g., *ndo-* 'try'). Table 1 shows the verb complex template in Potawatomi. Zero or more preverbs can appear in the preverb position as indicated by the asterisk. A reduplicant of the verb stem appears between any preverb and the verb stem.

Preverbs are their own prosodic words in Potawatomi. Lockwood states that "for the purpose of phonological rules, prenouns/preverbs are words" (2017:63), as "palatalization, syncope, and stress assignment do not cross prenoun/preverb boundaries" (2017:63n8).[4] Likewise, Hockett places marks in his fieldnotes that correspond roughly to word boundaries, including the boundary between a preverb and verb stem. Additionally, some first-language speakers of Potawatomi write preverbs as separate words or place a hyphen between the preverb and the verb stem.[5]

TABLE 1. Potawatomi verb complex template

INFLECTIONAL PREFIX-	PREVERB-*	STEM	-INFLECTIONAL SUFFIX(ES)
		[RED-initial-medial-final]	

Preverbs in Hockett 1948

Hockett (1948) tentatively proposes three distinct preverb positions. However, he notes in a footnote that "obviously the positional classification of some of the preverbs is entirely arbitrary. There is doubtless some technique, unknown to me in 1938–9, whereby such arbitrary assignment can be avoided" (1948:n3). I suspect the reason that Hockett was so apologetic in this quote was because he was working with insufficient data in 1938–39 when he wrote his dissertation. While Hockett did more fieldwork in 1940, his analysis in Hockett (1948) did not add data beyond that given in the dissertation. Hockett also had not yet edited Bloomfield's posthumous grammar of Menominee (Bloomfield 1962) that included an analysis of the preverb ordering in that language.

Hockett appears to have determined his ordering by listing a preverb in the first position if another preverb followed, and then making use of a third position only when it was necessary to account for a preverb that came after the ones that he had already placed in second position. This is what I believe he means by arbitrary, as such an analysis does not consider how all three preverbs are ordered with respect to each other. Table 2 gives Hockett's (1948) first three preverb positions.

There is evidence for an additional fourth position, designated as "inserted material" by Hockett (1948:141). This fourth position is not for preverbs, but for other material such as particles and/or nouns, after the third preverb position. Hockett claims that *wkéw* 'easily', *i* 'that', *wzhge* 'first time', as well as other words that are not part of the verb complex can occupy this position as shown in (2) (where preverbs are underlined).[6]

(2) (Hockett 1948:141)

a. wéj- kéw bigdebéshek
IC.why- easily break.head.VII.3
'why it breaks easily'

b. ga-gizh- i zhedé'at
IC.PST-after- that think.thus.VAI.3SG
'after he thought this thus'

c. é-gi- wzhge jizpenawat
C-PST- first.time pinch.VTA.3PL>3OBV
'they pinched him the first time'

TABLE 2. Hockett's 1948 ordering of preverbs

FIRST POSITION		SECOND POSITION		THIRD POSITION	
PREVERB	DEFINITION	PREVERB	DEFINITION	PREVERB	DEFINITION
a-	MOD	gi-	PST	ppich-	when, while, inasmuch
ge-	MOD	wi-	FUT.VOL	je-	where, while, how (means or manner)
ggo'-	quickly			we-	going to, on the way to, moving toward the place where such-and-such will be done
ndo-	try			gizh-	after, already
é-	C			ne-	when, then, until the time that
				wje-	why, toward
				zhe-	thus, so, how

d. wéj- ngom mégwa shakiyek yewat
IC.why- today still crawdads be.VAI.3PL
'why there are still crawdads today'

According to Hockett (1948), *wkéw* 'easily' in (2a), *i* 'that' in (2b), *wzhge* 'first time' in (2c), and *ngom* 'today', *mégwa* 'still', and *shakiyek* 'crawdads' in (2d) are not preverbs but particles and/or nouns that separate a preverb from the verb stem. Additionally, he notes that examples where this position occurs are all either conjunct order verbs or participles. While *i* 'that', *ngom* 'today', and *mégwa* 'still' are clearly not preverbs, as they show up as particles elsewhere in Hockett's field notes (see (3a) to (3c)), it is not clear why *wzhge* 'first time' is not considered a preverb because there are examples in Hockett's fieldnotes for which it is a preverb, as seen in (3d). Therefore, this paper treats it as a preverb. Note examples of *wkéw* 'easily' only show up in Hockett's field notes in this "fourth position."

(3) a. **i** je nemej na **i** mzen'egen.
that and not.know EMPH **that** paper
'And I don't know about the treaty.' (Hockett 1940a:5–6)

b. **ngom** ode wpi wémtegozhi yewak naganit.
today this time French be.VAI.3SG leader
'Up to this day, this French are the leaders somewhere.' (Hockett 1937:26)

c. mine **mégwa** ibe ngot bewak
and **still** there one sit.VAI.3SG
'There's still another one lying there.' (Hockett 1940c:52)

d. é-**wzhge**-mnokmek
C-**first.time**-be.spring.VII.3
'It is the beginning of springtime.' (Hockett 1940a:15)

Hockett discusses two other items under the header of preverb: negation and reduplication. He simply notes that the negative *bwa-* is the form of negation that shows up in the conjunct order and that it appears in at least one example after the past tense preverb. It is an anomaly that Hockett does not position it with the rest of the preverbs. I assume that this is because the negative *bwa-* has a different functional meaning than the preverbs in his third position. This paper treats it as a preverb. As for reduplication, Hockett outlines how it works and notes that it can convey "iteration, intensitivity, continuity, habitualness, or (at least in one case) inception" (1948:141). The reduplicant is positioned left adjacent to the verb stem. Hockett calls the reduplicant a "chameleon preverb" by which he means that the beginning of the verb stem determines the shape of the reduplicant. Hockett implies that nothing may intervene between the verb stem and the reduplicated prefix when he writes, "the phonemic shape of the chameleon preverb depends entirely on the morphophonemic shape of the beginning of the verb stem" (1948:141). Given the phonological unity with the verb stem, this paper does not treat the reduplicant as a preverb, in line with modern analyses of other Algonquian languages.

Corpus

The corpus consists of Charles Hockett's field notes from working with Potawatomi speakers Jim Alloway, Jim Spear, and Alice Spear from 1937 to 1940 in northern Wisconsin (Hockett 1939:preface). The speakers were all first-language speakers. These field notes contain four handwritten notebooks and several loose-leaf pages. The materials are archived in the California Language Archive at the University of California, Berkeley (Hockett 1937, 1940a,b,c). During the field work, the speakers told 74 narratives ranging from autobiographical to historical to traditional. The corpus contains 25,119 words, consisting of 6,951 unique words. I have typed up the materials, and I am currently editing them for accuracy. The data is relatively sparse, and as such, not every combination of preverbs is attested.

Preverb Inventory

In addition to the preverbs given in Hockett 1948, I referenced the Forest County Potawatomi dictionary (Forest County Potawatomi Community 2014) as I edited the preverbs in the corpus. The dictionary lists 60 preverbs. A complete list of the preverbs found there appears in Appendix 1. Several of these preverbs may be the same preverb, but with different meanings (e.g. *abje-* 'without stopping' and *yabje-* 'hurry'). It is an empirical question whether these and other doublets in Potawatomi are the same or different, but I do not answer the question in this paper due to insufficient semantic evidence.[7] Other preverbs listed in the dictionary are composed of multiple preverbs:

(4) bwamshe- 'before' > bwa- NEG and mshe- 'yet',
da-gi- 'should have' > da- MOD and gi- PST,
da-je- 'can; should' > da- MOD and je- MOD,
éche- 'the one who is doing that' > é- C and che- ?,
édso- 'so much, so many' > é- C and dso- 'so much, so many',
éshkwa- 'while, as long as' > é- C and shkwa- 'while, as long as'

Additionally, more preverbs appear in the corpus used in this paper that did not appear in the dictionary nor were listed by Hockett (1948). They came from Hockett's field notes that he had not analyzed before 1948. They appear in Appendix 2.

Overall Preverb Ordering

Methodology

I have standardized the way preverbs are represented in the corpus. Preverbs in the data are separated from the verb stem and each other by a hyphen. This allows me to target preverbs separately from initials that are sometimes homophonous with a preverb. Note the use of hyphens in the corpus is my own. As described above, there is no standardized way of writing preverbs.

Using Python (Rossum and Drake 2001), I read in the data as text files. I removed all special characters except hyphens. As is standard practice in computational linguistics, I did orthographic standardization; in this case undoing vowel lengthening of /w/ to /o/ as shown in (5):

(5) a. wd-o → wde-w
b. ndoch- → nde-wche-
c. -ozam- → e-wzam-
d. nm-oje- → nme-wje-

Standardization also adds a syncopated /e/ back into a preverb as shown in (6).

(6) a. -zh- → -zhe-
b. aj- → a-je-

I then did more orthographic standardization (e.g., to remove initial change from *wje-* < *wéj-*, to pick *bba-* over *pa-*, etc.).[8] Additionally, I exclude person prefixes, the complementizer *é-*, and tense markers with or without initial change from the subsequent analysis. I then looked for instances of two preverbs in a row using regular expressions in Python and pulled them out into a list. I break strings of three preverbs up into two pairs. There are no verb complexes in the data that contain more than three preverbs. Finally, I put all pairs of preverbs in a list.

Findings

I found 82 example types containing more than one preverb per verb complex. A very simple method to figure out the overall ordering of preverbs is to note the observed orders of three or more preverbs. There are three examples that contain more than two preverbs. These are given in (7). Note that *é-* is a complementizer. When it is present, it is the first element in a verb complex without exception, so it is not included in the analysis.

(7) a. é-bwa-yabje-bba-mdagwayyen
C-NEG-hurry-along-have.fun.VAI.2SG.CONJ
'Why don't you go have fun?' (Hockett 1940c:8)

b. é-bwa-mshe-nyéw-gongek
C-NEG-yet-four-order.of.day.VII.3.CONJ
'before four days were up' (Hockett 1939:17)

c. é-yé-bwa-wzam-naga'ayek
C-while-NEG-too.much-abuse.VTA.PASS.3.CONJ
'so he won't be too abused' (Hockett 1940a:78)

These three combinations yield the following partial ordering of preverbs:

(8) *yé-* 'while' > *bwa-* NEG > {{*mshe-* 'yet' > *nyéw-* 'four'}, {*yabje-* 'without stopping, hurry' > *bba-* 'around'}, *wzam-* 'too much'}

There may be more order in this set of preverbs, but the three combinations do not provide enough information to ascertain any further order.

However, if we look within combinations of all the preverbs, we can find order there. The results show that *gizh-* 'after, finish, already', *bnoj-* 'far off', and *yé-* 'while' are always ordered first in the pairs, and *kche-* 'really', *bba-* 'along', *ndo-* 'try', and *ko-* 'since' are always ordered second or third in the pairs, as shown for *gizh-* in (9a) and *ndo-* in (9b). Note that the examples in (9) contradict Hockett (1948).

(9) a. ga-gish-yabte-dbekek
IC.PST-after-half-be.night.VII.3
'after midnight' (Hockett 1940a:28)

b. w-gi-bme-ndo-babidgewan
3-PST-along-try-get.to.VTA.3SG>3OBV
'He went along trying to get at him.' (Hockett 1940c:5)

As there were still many other preverbs that are unaccounted for in the ordering above, I ran a simple sorting algorithm.[9] The search did not converge on a single order. There is one obvious issue that prevents the convergence of a single order, which I address next.

Topicalized Preverbs

Most problematic for a computational sort method, there are verbs that contain the same two preverbs in either order. The two relevant combinations would be *wje-* 'from, why'/*byé-* 'come' as shown in (10), and *wje-* 'from, why'/*bwa-* NEG as shown in (11).

(10) a. Kansas é-gi-**byé**-**wje**-majiyak.
Kansas C-PST-**come**-**from**-leave.VAI.1EXCL
'We came here from Kansas.' (Hockett 1940b:8)

b. wégni je wéj-byé-nanet ode nbenéshiyem.
what IC.why-come-get.VTA.2SG>3SG this my.bird.POSS
'Why have you come for my bird?' (Hockett 1940b:30)

(11) a. i je yé i o néné ga-bwa-wje-ntawét.
that DM PRED that that man IC.PST-NEG-why-kill.VAI.3SG
'That's why that man didn't kill (anything).' (Hockett 1937:53)

b. iw je yé i wéj-bwa-gkénmat
that DM PRED that IC.why-NEG-know.VTA.3SG>3OBV

wmezodan o mshiké.
his.parent.OBV that turtle
'That's why the turtle doesn't know his parents.' (Hockett 1940b:13)

One may think that there is a different position for the locational meaning of *wje-* 'from' verses the reason meaning of *wje-* 'why' in (10), but this does not hold up when comparing *wje-* in (10) to (11). Only the reason meaning of *wje-* 'why' is used in (11).

Research into other Algonquian languages suggests that one of the purported preverbs in each of these cases might actually be preverbs that have undergone movement to a position in the left of the clause. Dahlstrom (1995, 2000) finds in Meskwaki that the negative preverb *pwa·wi-* moves to a negative position and the oblique preverb *oči-* moves to a topic position resulting in two different orders of preverbs. Likewise, Shields (2005a) finds movement to a topic (or focus) position. However, unlike Dahlstrom, Shields argues that in Menominee adverbs, not preverbs, are the category that undergo movement to a topic (or focus) position.

These analyses of preverb ordering in other Algonquian languages suggest that the same phenomenon might be found in Potawatomi. Specifically, the preverb *wje-* in (10b) and (11b) is topicalized, but in (10a) and (11a) it is not. In Lewis (2015, 2016), I showed that Potawatomi has the following word order:

(12) Topic Negative Focus Verb {Subj, Obj, Obj2}

The topic position is where arguments that a sentence is about appear in the sentence. The negative position is for negative adverbs. The focus position is where arguments that are semantically asserted information appear. Subject, object, and second objects are unordered after the verb.

To better understand this process of topicalization, consider two things. First, focus clefts, like those in (11), are constructed with a participle. A participle in Potawatomi contains a verb: (1) conjugated in the conjunct order and (2) with an ablaut rule, known as initial change, applied to the first vowel of the verb (e.g., *wje-*, which contains an underlying weak vowel after the first consonant (*wEj-*), becomes *wéj-*). Second, *wje-* 'why' can be a topic in Potawatomi. I diagnose topics semantically following Reinhart 1982's definition that topics are what a sentence is about. As can be gleaned from (10b) and (11b), *wje-* is what the sentence is about. Note that *o néné* 'that man' is already in a topic position in (11a); this suggests why *wje-* does not move to a topic position.

Moreover, with topicalization in mind, it becomes clear for some of the data why there might be an interrupted position in Potawatomi, as pointed out in Hockett 1948 (Hockett's implied "fourth preverb position"). The preverb likely has moved to a topic position allowing a demonstrative or particle to appear to the right of it and before the rest of the verb complex as shown in (13). The particles *i* 'that' and *mine* 'again' follow the preverb *wéch-*/*wéj-*, which is in a topic position.

(13) a. wéch- i kedot?
IC.why- that say.thus.VAI.3SG
'Why does she say that?' (Hockett 1940b:14)

b. wéj- mine nim'ediwat
IC.why- again dance.VAI.3PL
'why they were dancing again' (Hockett 1940b:21)

Finally, note that the topicalized *wéch* is not a particle in (10b) and (11b). We can tell that it is not a particle because the verb would have initial change or *é-* on it if *wéch* were a particle. It is important to note here that the initial change form of *byé-* 'come' and *bwa-* NEG are indistinguishable from their non–initial change forms.

Returning to the analysis, I again ran the sort algorithm on the data this time without the topicalized preverbs. Although the sort fared better (it showed less variation in orders), it still did not converge on a single ordering. I found 79 example types containing more than one preverb per verb. I plot these pairs of combinations in Table 3. The combinations are plotted by alphabetical order of the first preverb and no particular order of the second preverb. The token count of attested examples is given in the table cells.

The upshot of this section is that preverbs do have some relative orderings, but based on the corpus data there is no clear overall ordering. While an overall ordering cannot be found, I can order preverbs that are currently not ordered with respect to each other by grouping preverbs by semantic class, as Cook (2003) attempted to do for Menominee. I turn to this approach next.

Ordering by Semantic Classes

Cook 2003

Cook (2003) proposed four major semantic categories for Menominee preverbs: MODAL, which contains pure modal preverbs (e.g., *aw-* IRR), control preverbs (e.g., *katāew-* DES), or preverbs of the outcomes of an attempt (e.g., *puaq-* 'fail to'); ASPECT, which contains aspectual preverbs that pick out endpoints of an event (e.g., *kēs-* COMP), the internal structure of an event (e.g. *māek-* PROG), or temporal ordering of events (e.g., *nawāc-* 'before, first'); SPATIAL, which contains directed motion preverbs (e.g., *pes-* 'coming') or spatial orientation preverbs (e.g., *wāeh-* 'at a distance'); and ADVERB, which contains preverbs of manner (e.g., *es-* 'thus') and degree (e.g., *kāeqc-* 'really').

Cook (2003) also claimed that Menominee preverbs follow an ordering by semantic class, as shown in (14):

(14) MODAL > ASPECT > SPATIAL > ADVERB

However, Kline et al. (2025) show that this relative order does not work for Menominee, saying "Cook's work served as a useful first discussion and classification of the semantics of Menominee preverbs, but her two claims about their ordering and constraints on that ordering do not hold up against a larger corpus." Regardless of the empirical adequacy of Cook 2003, it suggests a strategy that can be applied to Potawatomi.

The following semantic classification emerges in Potawatomi: the first category is SUBORD, which houses a number of subordinating preverbs that require the conjunct *bwa-*, *gizh-*, and *yé-*. Note that *gizh-* 'finish, after' is subordinate and aspectual. Only the subordinating function forces the conjunct. SUBORD does not contain control preverbs. SPATIAL contains spatial preverbs as in Cook 2003.

TABLE 3. Preverb combinations (first preverb on the y-axis, second preverb on the x-axis)

	dzhe-	bzhe-	bon-	déb-	kche-	mno-	ndo-	nizh-	je-	wzam-	bba-	byé-	gzhge-	mshe-	mje-	wje-	yabje-	zhe-	bidgé-	wzhge-	bme-	bwa-	nme-	jak-	yabte-	mdadso-	ngot-	wizh-	ko-	kwé-	pij-	se-	wzhe-	gwin-	nkwé-	wkéw-
zhe-					1	1							1																							
yé-					2																1															
yabje-											1																									
wje-					1	2						1										2	1													1
wéb-					1																															
we-					3	1			2		1							1													1			1	1	
nme-			2	1	1	1				1		1				1		2						1					1	1	1	1	1			
ndo-						1																														
ko-																										1	1									
kche-																												1								
gizh-									1												1	1	1	1	5											
byé-					1				2							10		5	1	1																
bwa-				2		2				1		1	3	9	1	1	1	1																		
bnoj-											1																									
bme-	1		1	1	3	1	1	1	1	1																										
bbi-		1																																		
bba-	1																																			

ASPECT contains aspectual preverbs as in Cook 2003. Finally, ADVERB contains adverb preverbs as in Cook 2003 as well as control preverbs.

(15) Semantic categories for Potawatomi

a. SUBORD

Subordinators: bwa- NEG/IRR, gizh- 'after', yé- 'while', pich- 'while', ko- 'since'

b. SPATIAL

Directed motion: bme- 'along'/bba- 'around', byé- 'come'/nme- 'getting to be, away', byé- 'come'/we- 'go'

Spatial orientation: dzhe-/je- 'in a certain location', wje- 'from', bnoj- 'far off', bidgé- 'enter', bij- 'in'

c. ASPECT

Endpoints of an event: wéb- 'start', bon- 'stop', gizh- 'after, finish, already', ne- 'getting to be'

Internal structure of an event: nta- 'always', kwé- 'for a while', yabje- 'without stopping'

Temporal ordering of events: wzhge- 'first time', nkwé- 'first', ko- 'since', mshe- 'yet'

d. ADVERB

Manner: ne-/zhe- 'thus, how', mno- 'good', mje- 'bad', wizh- 'strong', kew- 'easily', pche- 'by accident', gzhe- 'quickly', wkéw- 'easily', ggo'- 'suddenly', wzhe- 'order',

Degree: kche- 'really', yabje- 'hurry', wzam- 'too much', bbi-/pich- 'so much', numerals (ngot- 'one', etc.), jak- 'all'

Control: ndo- 'try', gzhge- 'be able to', déb- 'have a chance to', gwin- 'unable'

Emphasis: bzhe- EMPH, se- ?

I then ran a computational sort method on the semantic classes. The findings are summarized in Table 4. Each shaded cell in Table 4 shows combinations of preverbs within the same semantic class. The most frequent class to have more than one preverb is the spatial class. I do not make any predictions that would restrict more than one preverb in a semantic class appearing together. In fact, there may be ordering of preverbs within each semantic class. I leave this to future research to solve.

Additionally, the combinations of preverbs to the left of the shaded cells in Table 4 are the topicalized preverbs in (10b) and (11b), as well as a hard to analyze instance of *yabje-* 'without stopping, hurry', which can be adverbial and aspectual.

TABLE 4. Semantic ordered preverb combinations (first preverb on the y-axis, second preverb on the x-axis)

		yabje-	bwa-	byé-	je-	wje-	bme-	nme-	nkwé-	dzhe-	bba-	bidgé-	mshe-	bon-	wzhge-	ko-	kwé-	mdadso-	ngot-	gzhge-	ndo-	déb-	mno-	mje-	wzam-	zhe-	jak-	kche-	nizh-	wzhe-	pij-	se-	gwin-	bzhe-	wizh-	yabte-	wkéw-
ADVERB	kche-																																		1		
	bbi-																																	1			
	zhe-																			1			1					1									
	wje-		1	1																			2					1									1
	ndo-																						1														
ASPECT	wéb-																											1									
	ko-																	1	1																		
	yabje-										1																										
SPATIAL	nme-			1		1								2		1	1					1	1		1	2	1	1		1	1	1					
	byé-				2	10						1			1											5		1								5	
	bnoj-										1																										
	bme-				1					1				1							1	1	1		1			3	1								
	bba-									1																											
	we-				2				1		1												1			1		3			1		1				
SUBORD	yé-						1																					2									
	gizh-		1		1		1	1																			1									1	
	bwa-	1		1		1							9							3		2	2	1	1	1											
		SUBORD		SPATIAL									ASPECT					ADVERB																			

It is unclear which meaning it has in the example in (16), but I have categorized it as if it were aspectual.

(16) é-bwa-yabje-bba-mdagwayyen.
C-NEG-hurry/without.stopping-go.around-have.fun.VAI.2SG
'Why don't you go have fun?' (Hockett 1940b:8)

The ordering found by sorting the data by the four semantic classes is as follows:

(17) SUBORD > SPATIAL > ASPECT > ADVERB

Thus, Potawatomi preverbs can be given the ordering in (17) based on four semantic categories.

Hockett 1948

While some of Hockett's claims cannot be evaluated because of a lack of data, the findings in this paper largely contradict Hockett 1948.[10] First, the preverb *ndo-* 'try' can appear after *bme-* 'along' (and the past tense preverb *gi-*) as shown in (18a). Second, the preverb *é-* is not in the same position as *ndo-* 'try' as it can appear before *ndo-* in (18b). Finally, the preverbs *gizh-*, *we-*, *wje-*, and *zhe-* can have preverbs after them. Therefore, they are not the closest preverb to the verb stem.

(18) a. w-gi-bme-ndo-babidgewan
3-PST-along-try-get.to.VTA.3SG>3OBV
'He went along trying to get at him.' (Hockett 1940c:5)

b. é-gi-ndo-nsegot
C-PST-try-kill.VTA.3OBV>3SG
'he tried to kill him' (Hockett 1940b:31)

Thus, Hockett's analysis largely does not hold up to closer investigation and can be replaced with the semantic class order proposed in this paper.

Future Research

More research remains to be done. First, the corpus needs to be enlarged, for example, by adding religious texts as noted in Lewis 2023.

Second, although I addressed movement of preverbs to a topic position, the semantic combinations of preverbs and the verb stem need to be better understood more generally. Slavin (2005) argues that in addition to a semifixed preverb order, a scope principle is responsible for the ordering of preverbs. This needs to be explored for Potawatomi, particularly with respect to *yabje-* 'without stopping, hurry' and *gizh-* 'after, finish, already'. Additionally, are position and meaning tied together for some preverbs? For example, can *gizh-* 'after, finish, already' or *yabje-* 'without stopping, hurry' appear in more than one position? It is possible cross-linguistically. Slavin (2005) has found that the cognate preverb *nihtaa-* 'like to, be good at' in Oji-Cree changes meanings depending on if it is in a preverb position or an initial position. She finds this to be the case for *ishkwaa-* 'after, finish' as well, which she says occupies two different classes (Slavin 2005:19–20). Semantic fieldwork holds the answers to whether these facts are also true for Potawatomi.

Finally, there is a growing body of literature on preverb orderings in Algonquian languages (Dahlstrom 1995, 2000; Valentine 2001; Shields 2005a,b; Rhodes 2005; Slavin 2005; Kline et al. 2025). The analysis here would benefit from a more in-depth comparison of these works.

Conclusion

This paper replaces Hockett's (1948) arbitrary positional ordering of preverbs. I have shown that an overall ordering of preverbs in Potawatomi is not possible given the corpus, but one is possible for Potawatomi using four semantic classes. This paper also shows that with good data in plain text formats, a few simple computational tools and methods can be leveraged to do the work of language reclamation.

Appendix 1: Preverbs in Forest County Potawatomi Community (2014)

abje- 'without stopping'
ano- 'repeatedly'

bapne- ‘confused, all over the place’
bba-/pa- ‘about, around’
bme- ‘along, around, by, past’
bon- ‘quit, finish’
bwa- ‘no, not (used to negate with conjunct verbs); least’
bwa-mshe-/bwamshe- ‘before’
byé- ‘here, this way; come’
da- ‘will; can; could; might; should, ought to’
da-gi- ‘should have’
da-je- ‘can; should’
dé-/déb- ‘able to’
dép- ‘enough, sufficient; able to succeed’
dgo- ‘in with, along with, added in’
é- ‘factive’
éche- ‘the one who is doing that’
édso- ‘so much, so many’
éshkwa- ‘while, as long as’
étso- ‘every’
ge- ‘future tense (will)’
gge- ‘with, along with’
gi- ‘past tense’
gimoch- ‘sneak, sneaky’
gizh-/gish- ‘finish, done; already; after’
gwékme- ‘past (a certain time)’
gwiyash-/gweyash- ‘already mistakenly (have done something)’
gwje- ‘try’
jag-/jak- ‘all, everything’
je-/éje- ‘in a certain place; there, the place where’
kche- ‘a lot; really’
(w)kéw- ‘prone; easily’
kwé-/kewé- ‘for a while, a little while’
mamwe-/mamo- ‘all, greatest, most’
mche- ‘unaided; freely (of one’s own free will)’
mno- ‘fine, good, well’
naj- ‘go after, fetch’
ndo- ‘try, attempt’

nme- 'along, away, by; must have'
nondé- 'too soon'
npe- 'as well as, along with'
nshiw- 'really, very much, a lot'
nshkaj- 'in anger'
nta- 'like to do something a lot'
o-/we- 'go, go over in order to, go and'
pche- 'by mistake; accidently'
pich-/épich-/épit- 'such an extent; still; meanwhile'
wéb-/wép- 'start'
wi- 'future tense (want to, be going to, will)'
wige- 'carefully'
wje- 'from; for the reason that'
wzhge-/wshke- 'new, for the first time; early'
yabje- 'hurry'
zhe-/ézh- 'a certain way'

Appendix 2: Additional Preverbs in Spear-Alloway Corpus

bbi- 'such an extent'
bidgé- 'enter'
bij- in
bnoj- 'far off'
bzhe- EMPH
déb- 'chance to'
dzhe- 'in a certain location'
ggo'- 'suddenly'
gwin- 'unable'
gzhge- 'able to'
jak- 'all'
je- 'in a certain location'
ko- 'since'
mdatso- 'ten'
mje- 'bad'
mshe- 'yet'

ne- 'getting to be'
ngot- 'one'
nizh- 'two'
nkwé- 'first'
se- ?
wizh- 'really'
wkéw- 'easily'
wzam- 'too much'
wzhe- 'order'
yé- 'while'

NOTES

1. I would like to thank Dustin Bowers, Hunter Lockwood, Lindsay Marean, my reviewers and the editorial team, and the participants at the 55th Algonquian Conference for their suggestions.
2. Note that Kline et al. (2025) find that Cook (2003) does not hold for a larger data set.
3. The orthography used in this paper is the Wisconsin Native American Languages Program orthography (Daniels and Daniels 1976): a=[a], i=[i], o=[o], é=[æ], e=[ə], sh=[ʃ], zh=[ʒ], '=[ʔ], j=[dʒ], and ch=[tʃ]. The abbreviations used in this paper are the following: C = complementizer, COMP = completive, CONJ = conjunct, DES = desiderative, DM = discourse marker, EMPH = emphasis, EXCL = exclusive, FUT.VOL = future volitional, IC = initial change, IRR = irrealis, MOD = modal, NEG = negation, OBV = obviative, PL = plural, PASS = passive, POSS = possessive, PRED = predicate, PROG = progressive, PST = past, RED = reduplication, SG = singular, SUBORD = subordinating, VAI = animate intransitive verb, VII = inanimate intransitive verb, VTA = transitive animate verb, 1 = first person, 2 = second person, 3 = third person, > = acts on.
4. Preverbs in other Algonquian languages have similar properties (see, e.g., Russell 1999 on Cree; Miller 2018 on Saulteaux).
5. This has become the convention in the traditional writing system, Wisconsin Native American Languages Program's writing system, and the learners writing system. However, in the Prairie Band Potawatomi Nation's writing system one writes preverbs and the verb stem together as a single orthographic word.
6. Hockett (1948:141) lists the form *kéw* 'easily', but it is written in his field notes with a /w/ before it as *wkéw* (Hockett 1937).
7. As pointed out to me by Hunter Lockwood, the deep history of Potawatomi

multilingualism (Ojibwe, Fox, Sauk, and Kickapoo) may be relevant in cases where there is a doublet.

8. The rest of the changes to achieve orthographic standardization are: *gish-* → *gizh-*, *go-* → *ko-*, *nbyé-* → *mbyé-*, *wbem-* → *bme-*, *wép-* → *wéb-*, *wéj-* → *wéch-*, *wéch-* → *wj-*, *-o-* → *-we-*, *o-* → *we-*, *ne-* → *nme-*, *gwi-* → *gwin-*, *dép-* → *déb-*, *gshg-* → *gzhg-*, *zhi-* → *zhe-*, *mne-* → *mno-*.
9. Specifically, I used a bubble sort, or sorting by exchange, method that repeatedly compares two adjacent elements in a list (Friend 1956).
10. One example of Hockett's lack of data is that *ggo'-* 'quickly' does not show up in a lexical preverb combination in the corpus. Hockett (1948:140) only found it with a person prefix.

REFERENCES

Bloomfield, Leonard. 1962. *The Menomini Language*, ed. by Charles. F. Hockett. New Haven: Yale University Press.

Cook, Clare. 2003. A Semantic Classification of Menominee Preverbs. *Papers of the Thirty-Fourth Algonquian Conference*, ed. by H. C. Wolfart, pp. 35–56. Winnipeg: University of Manitoba. https://ojs.library.carleton.ca/index.php/ALGQP/article/view/396/300.

Dahlstrom, Amy. 1995. *Topic, Focus, and Other Word Order Problems in Algonquian*. The Belcourt Lecture, Delivered before the University of Manitoba on 25 February 1994. Winnipeg: Voice of Rupert's Land.

Dahlstrom, Amy. 2000. Morphosyntactic Mismatches in Algonquian: Affixal Predicates and Discontinuous Verbs. *Proceedings of CLS 36*, ed. by Arika Okrent and John P. Boyle, pp. 63–87. Chicago: Chicago Linguistic Society.

Daniels, Billy, and Mary Daniels. 1976. *An Introduction to Wisconsin Potawatomi*, ed. by John Nichols. University of Wisconsin–Milwaukee. Wisconsin Native American Language Project.

Forest County Potawatomi Community. 2014. *Ézhe-bmadzimgek gdebodwéwadmi-zheshmomenan: Potawatomi Dictionary*. Crandon: Forest County Potawatomi Community.

Friend, Edward H. 1956. Sorting on Electronic Computer Systems. *Journal of the ACM* 3(3):134–168.

Goddard, Ives. 1975. Algonquian, Wiyot, and Yurok: Proving a Distant Genetic Relationship. *Linguistics and Anthropology in Honor of C. F. Voegelin*, ed. by M. Dale Kinkade, Kenneth L. Hale, and Otmar Werner, pp. 249–262. Lisse: Peter De Ridder Press.

Goddard, Ives. 1990. Aspects of the Topic Structure of Fox Narratives: Proximate Shifts and the Use of Overt and Inflectional NPs. *International Journal of American Linguistics*

56(3):317–340.

Hockett, Charles F. 1937. Hockett Potawatomi Field Notebook 4, Welcher.002.004. *Laura Buszard-Welcher Papers on the Potawatomi Language*. California Language Archive, University of California, Berkeley. http://dx.doi.org/doi:10.7297/X2QC022K.

Hockett, Charles F. 1939. The Potawatomi Language. PhD thesis, Yale University.

Hockett, Charles F. 1940a. Hockett Potawatomi Field Notebook 1, Welcher.002.001. *Laura Buszard-Welcher Papers on the Potawatomi Language*. California Language Archive, University of California, Berkeley. http://dx.doi.org/doi:10.7297/X23J3BH0.

Hockett, Charles F. 1940b. Hockett Potawatomi Field Notebook 2, Welcher.002.002. *Laura Buszard-Welcher Papers on the Potawatomi Language*. California Language Archive, University of California, Berkeley. http://dx.doi.org/doi:10.7297/X2ZW1JGG.

Hockett, Charles F. 1940c. Hockett Potawatomi Field Notebook 3, Welcher.002.003. *Laura Buszard-Welcher Papers on the Potawatomi Language*. California Language Archive, University of California, Berkeley. http://dx.doi.org/doi:10.7297/X2V40SSH.

Hockett, Charles F. 1948. Potawatomi III: The Verb Complex. *International Journal of American Linguistics* 14(3):139–149. https://doi.org/10.1086/463995.

Kline, Andrew, Monica Macaulay, and Jennifer Stoughton. 2025. Menominee Preverb Ordering Revisited. *Papers of the Fifty-Fourth Algonquian Conference*, ed. by Inge Genee, Monica Macaulay, and Natalie Weber, pp. 149-168. East Lansing: Michigan State University Press.

Lewis, Robert E., Jr. 2015. Determining that Potawatomi Word Order Is Pragmatically Conditioned. Paper read at the 47th Algonquian Conference, University of Manitoba.

Lewis, Robert E., Jr. 2016. Information Structure Conditioned Word Order in Potawatomi. Paper read at the 42nd Annual Meeting of the Society for the Study of the Indigenous Languages of the Americas, Washington, DC.

Lewis, Robert E., Jr. 2023. A Survey of Computational Infrastructure to Help Preserve and Revitalize Bodwéwadmimwen. *Proceedings of the Sixth Workshop on the Use of Computational Methods in the Study of Endangered Languages*, ed. by Atticus Harrigan, Aditi Chaudhary, Shruti Rijhwani, Sarah Moeller, Antti Arppe, Alexis Palmer, Ryan Henke, Daisy Rosenblum, pp. 44–50. Baltimore: Association for Computational Linguistics. https://aclanthology.org/2023.computel-1.7.

Lockwood, Hunter Thompson. 2017. How the Potawatomi Language Lives: A Grammar of Potawatomi. PhD thesis, University of Wisconsin–Madison.

Miller, Taylor Lampton. 2018. The Phonology-Syntax Interface and Polysynthesis: A Study of Kiowa and Saulteaux Ojibwe. PhD thesis, University of Delaware.

Reinhart, Tanya. 1982. Pragmatics and Linguistics: An Analysis of Sentence Topics. *Philosophica* 27(1):53–94.

Rhodes, Richard A. 2005. Directional Preverbs in Ojibwe and the Registration of Path. *Papers of the Thirty-Sixth Algonquian Conference*, ed. by H. C. Wolfart, pp. 371–382. Winnipeg: University of Manitoba. https://ojs.library.carleton.ca/index.php/ALGQP/article/view/365/269.

Rossum, Guido van, and Fred. L. Drake (eds.). 2001. *Python Reference Manual.* Reston: PythonLabs.

Russell, Kevin. 1999. The "Word" in Two Polysynthetic Languages. *Studies on the Phonological Word*, ed. by Alan T. Hall and Ursula Kleinhenz, pp. 203–222. Amsterdam: John Benjamins.

Shields, Rebecca. 2005a. The Functional Hierarchy in Menominee: Preverbs and Adverbs. *Proceedings from the Annual Meeting of the Chicago Linguistic Society* 4:431–444. Chicago: Chicago Linguistic Society.

Shields, Rebecca. 2005b. Menominee Preverbs as Functional Categories. *Papers of the Thirty-Sixth Algonquian Conference*, ed. by H. C. Wolfart, pp. 383–406. Winnipeg: University of Winnipeg. https://ojs.library.carleton.ca/index.php/ALGQP/article/view/366/270.

Slavin, Tanya. 2005. Preverb Ordering in Ojibwe. MA thesis, University of Toronto.

Valentine, J. Randolph. 2001. *Nishnaabemwin Reference Grammar*. Toronto: University of Toronto Press.

Semantic Effects of Two VII Finals and a New Diagnostic for Medials as Verbal Classifiers in Ojibwe

Cherry Meyer and Anna Whitney

Traditionally, Algonquian words are analyzed as consisting of an initial and a final, with a potential intermediate component called a medial (Bloomfield 1946; Goddard 1990).[1]

Many medials occur phonologically unchanged across different parts of speech, e.g., nouns (1) and verbs (2). Medials have been categorized in different ways, for example, by semantic properties, e.g. environmental medials (Valentine 2001:332) or body-part medials (Valentine 2001:330, 386), or by morphosyntactic properties, e.g., incorporated medials (Valentine, 2001:330) or classificatory medials (Valentine 2001:331).

(1) nabagaabikoon
    nabag- aabik -w -an
    flat- rock -N -PL.AN
    'flat rocks'

(2) nibiiw- aabik -aa
    wet- rock -be.VII
    'there is wet rock'

In Ojibwe (Algonquian), there are two Inanimate Intransitive verb (VII) finals with forms *-aa* and *-ad* that share the meaning 'it is in a state or condition', which we gloss for the sake of space as 'be'. With a choice between these two VII finals, some medials occur only with the verb final *-aa*, some occur only with *-ad*, and some occur with both. We find that medials occurring with *-aa* exhibit incorporation-like entity semantics, while those occurring with *-ad* exhibit classifier-like quality semantics.

In a detailed study of incorporated and classifier medials in Ojibwe, Whitney et al. (2023) evaluate the incorporated or classifier status of medials on three diagnostics, including semantics, argument role, and whether the medial could co-occur with an overt noun. Regarding semantics, they sort medials according to incorporation-like entity semantics and classifier-like quality semantics. Incorporated medials denote an object or otherwise concrete thing in the world, for example, a rock or firewood. In contrast, classifiers express qualities such as material and shape, for example, mineral (3) or berry-like (4).

(3) gaash- aabik -ad
sharp- mineral -be.VAI
'it (something mineral) is sharp'

(4) misko- minag -ad
red- berry.like -be.VII
'it (globular) is red'

This semantic distinction is especially evident in medials that may express either entity or quality semantics, for example, *-aabik-* 'rock; mineral (stone, glass, metal)', with the former being expressed with *-aa* (5) and the latter with *-ad* (6).

(5) nibiiw- aabik -aa
wet- rock -be.VII
'there is wet rock'

(6) nibiiw- aabik -ad
wet- mineral -be.VII
'it (something mineral) is wet'

Further, medials occurring with *-ad* may co-occur with an overt noun, which is a robust diagnostic for classifier status. In order to better understand what governs the use of VII finals *-aa* versus *-ad*, as well as whether the choice between these two finals might prove a useful diagnostic for distinguishing incorporated from classifier medials, we investigate a broad set of medials occurring with these finals. Occurrence with *-ad* is shown to be a reliable diagnostic for classifier status.

An additional and related pattern emerges, in which verbs containing medials in combination with the final *-aa* express existential semantics (7), that is, 'there is X' or 'there are X', while verbs with medials in combination with *-ad* express predicative semantics (8), that is, 'it is X' or 'it has X'.

(7) bengo- jiishkiwag -aa
dry- mud -be.VII
'there is dry mud'

(8) bengo- jiishkiwag -ad
dry- mud.like -be.VII
'it (something mud-like) is dry'

We outline our methods and the background of the project before discussing the semantic effects of these VII finals on medials. We first present several medials showing entity semantics that occur with *-aa* and are nonclassificatory. We then present medials showing quality semantics that occur with *-ad* and are clearly classifiers, followed by medials that express entity semantics with *-aa* and quality semantics with *-ad*. Then, we move on to the patterns of existential and predicative verbal semantics expressed with *-aa* and *-ad*, respectively. We discuss effects of animacy, issues for morpheme identity, and the relationship between medials and finals, and compare to a previous analysis before concluding and identifying areas for further research.

Methods and Background

Medials, verbs, and examples for this project are drawn from the online *Ojibwe People's Dictionary* (2021, *OPD*). The *OPD* is composed of words from 16 communities in Wisconsin, Minnesota, and north of the Canadian border in Ontario and Manitoba. The varieties commonly labeled Southwestern and Saulteaux are spoken in these communities. We also consulted Valentine's *Nishnaabemwin Reference Grammar*, which covers the Eastern and Odawa varieties, and found the same patterns.[2]

While we know classifiers occur as medials, combining this Algonquianist tradition with current approaches to classifier typology requires some translation.

Crosslinguistically, classifiers are defined as free or bound morphemes occurring in specifiable morphosyntactic units that denote a property of the referent of a noun and may co-occur with that noun (Aikhenvald 2000:13; Grinevald 2000:64). SPECIFIABLE MORPHOSYNTACTIC UNITS means that classifiers are labeled according to the part of speech to which they are adjacent or attached (Aikhenvald 2000:13; Grinevald 2000:62–63). For example, verbal classifiers are attached to verbs and numeral classifiers are attached or adjacent to numerals. This typology was developed to distinguish different types of classifiers, both across and within languages (Grinevald 2000:58).

Ojibwe has both numeral and verbal classifiers (Meyer 2020:43), making it a MULTIPLE CLASSIFIER language (Aikhenvald 2000:205). While some classifier medials occur as both verbal and numeral classifiers, the sets are not identical (Meyer 2020:48–49). We focus here on verbal classifiers, that is, classifier medials in verbs. While these have been discussed using the terms CLASSIFICATORY MEDIALS, NOUN CLASSIFIERS, and CLASSIFIER MEDIALS (Valentine 2001:330–332), we prefer classifier medials, in order to make clear their crosslinguistic status.

Biedny et al. (2021) provide a survey of verbal classifiers across the Algonquian family, noting that it is common for Algonquianists to distinguish multiple kinds of medials (Biedny et al. 2021:4), though there are various labels and diagnostics employed. Generally researchers sort medials into at least two categories, with one category containing classifiers or classificatory medials and the other category representing body-part medials, common medials, incorporating medials, and other terms. Biedny et al. utilize the term INCORPORATED MEDIALS to encompass the wide variety of nonclassifier medials, which we follow.

In terms of semantic function, the label of incorporated medials is useful in drawing a parallel between incorporated nouns and nonclassifier medials on the one hand, and a contrast between those and classifier medials on the other. Noun incorporation is a detransitivizing process that combines an independent noun and verb to create a new verb (Mithun 1986). Herein, we discuss only incorporation of object nouns. Compare the transitive verb with an independent noun in (9) to the intransitive verb with the incorporated noun in (10). The independent noun in the former refers to specific potatoes, while the incorporated noun in the latter does not refer to specific potatoes; rather, it limits the scope of the verb to a certain kind of digging, that is, that having to do with potatoes, and might thus be translated as 'potato-dig'. Incorporated nouns and incorporated medials do not refer to specific entities, as independent nouns do, though both are nominal in nature, that is, they refer to entities. Classifiers do not refer to entities; they add or highlight particular qualities of entities.

(9) Mii iw gii- **moon** **-a'w** -aad
it.is DEM.IN.SG PST- dig -VTA.act.on.AN.with.tool -3.SG>3'
iniw odoo- **pinii** -man.
DEM.AN.OBV 3.SG.POSS- potato -OBV
'He dug up his potatoes'

(10) moon**hapnii**
moonah- **apiny** -e
dig.for- potato -VAI
'dig for potatoes' (Valentine 2001:410)

In the process of distinguishing incorporated medials from classifier medials, Whitney et al. (2023) notice that VIIs occurring with the final *-aa* and without a medial (11–12) instead occur with final *-ad* when a medial is present (13–14) (see also Valentine 2001:345–347).

(11) dakw- aa
short- be.VII
'it is short'

(12) ginw- aa
long- be.VII
'it is long'

(13) dakoo- sag -ad
short- useful.wood -be.VII
'it (useful wood) is short'

(14) ginw- aakw -ad
long- stick.like -be.VII
'it (stick-like) is long'

Further examination reveals that the pattern is more complex, such that both verb finals are overwhelmingly more likely to occur with a medial than without, as shown in Table 1.

In the following section, we first provide examples of incorporated medials that occur with the VII final *-aa* and only express entity semantics.

TABLE 1. VIIs occurring with finals *-aa* and *-ad*

VERB FINAL TOTAL	*-aa* 379	*-ad* 364
Occurs with medial	298 (78.6%)	338 (92.9%)
Occurs without medial	81 (21.4%)	26 (7.1%)

Medials Expressing Entity Semantics with -aa and Quality Semantics with *-ad*

Stable Occurrence with VII Final -aa and Entity Semantics

Some medials, notably of the semantic group of ENVIRONMENTAL MEDIALS (Valentine 2001:332, 365–371) always show entity semantics, and as such, only occur with VII final *-aa*. To be clear, we mean that between the choice of the VII finals *-aa* or *-ad*, these medials only occur with *-aa*, though they may certainly occur with finals other than *-aa* and *-ad*. Some examples include *-adin-* 'hill' (15–16), *-kob-* 'brush (vegetation)' (17–18), and *-aagonag-* 'snow (on the ground)' (19–20).[3] These are incorporated medials that are disallowed from occurring with overt nouns. Given that intransitive verbs can only take subjects and these environmental medials often occur in verbs with impersonal subjects, such as weather or landforms, the lack of overt nouns is not surprising. Valentine (2001:365) provides a disallowed example for *-aagonag-* 'snow (on the ground)' (21).

(15) giji- adin -aa
jagged- hill -be.VII
'there is a range of hills, a ridge'

(16) agas- adin -aa
small- hill -be.VII
'there is a small hill'

(17) biko- kob -aa
lump- brush -be.VII
'it is a clump of brush'

(18) dabas- kob -aa
low- brush -be.VII
'it is low brush'

(19) a. bagak- aagonag -aa
bright- snow -be.vii
'there is bright snow'

(20) ishp- aagonag -aa
high- snow -be.VII
'it is deep snow'

(21) *Shp- aagnag -aa maanda ki.
high- snow -VII.be this.IN.SG land.IN.SG
Intended: 'This land is deep in snow.'

Stable Occurrence with VII Final -ad and Quality Semantics

Certain medials always show quality semantics and occur only with VII final *-ad*. Examples include the medials *-(i)g-* 'wood' (22),[4] *-aad-* 'way of being, life' (23–24), *-iig-* or *-eg-* 'sheetlike' (25–26),[5] *-minag-* 'berrylike' (27–28), and *-aabiig-* 'stringlike' (29–30). These are all classifier medials that may co-occur with overt nouns as subject.

(22) mashkaw- ig -ad
strong/hard- wood -be.VII
'it is strong, hard wood'

(23) maan- aad -ad
bad- way.of.being -be.VII
'it is bad, is no good, is ugly'

(24) nook- aad -ad
soft- way.of.being -be.VII
'it is mild'

(25) agaas- iig -ad
small- sheet.like -be.VII
'it (sheetlike) is small'

(26) apiich- iig -ad
to.a.certain.extent- sheet.like -be.VII
'it (sheetlike) has a certain thickness'

(27) biisi- minag -ad
fine- berry.like -be.VII
'it (small and round) is fine'

(28) misko- minag -ad
red- berry.like -be.VII
'it (small and round, grain, berry) is red'

(29) baapas- aabiig -ad
tight- string.like -be.VII
'it (stringlike) is tight, is taut'

(30) baabiikw- aabiig -ad
lumps- string.like -be.VII
'it (stringlike) has knots, has lumps in it'

Medials Occurring with -aa Showing Entity Semantics and -ad Showing Quality Semantics

The next set of medials may exhibit either entity or quality semantics. These medials may be incorporated and show entity semantics with the VII final *-aa*, or may function as verbal classifiers showing quality semantics with the VII final *-ad*. It should be noted that these medials may also show entity and quality semantics with verb finals other than the VII finals *-aa* and *-ad*. The first medial exhibiting the entity semantics (31–32) and quality semantics (33–34) is *-aabik-* 'rock; mineral substance (inorganic solid: rock, metal, glass)'.

(31) nibiiw- aabik -aa
wet- rock -be.VII
'there is wet rock'

(32) gaash- aabik -aa
sharp- rock -be.VII
'there is sharp, rough rock'

(33) nibiiw- aabik -ad
wet- mineral -be.VII
'it (something mineral) is wet'

(34) gaash- aabik -ad
sharp- mineral -be.VII
'it (mineral) is sharp'

The second medial exhibiting entity (35–36) and quality semantics (37–38) is *-aak(w)-* 'woods, forest, trees; sticklike, wood'.

(35) akw- aakw -aa
a.certain.length- woods -be.VII
'the woods go a certain distance'

(36) gashkii- dibik- aak -aa
completely.covered- night- forest -be.VII
'the forest is dark'

(37) akw- aakw -ad
a.certain.length- stick.like -be.VII
'it (sticklike, wood) is so long, is so tall'

(38) bengw- aakw -ad
dry- stick.like -be.VII
'it (sticklike) is dry'

The third medial exhibiting the entity (39–40) and quality semantics (41–42) is -(*i*)*sag*- 'floor, room; useful or worked wood'.

(39) nibiiw- isag -aa
wet- floor -be.VII
'the floor is wet'

(40) ginoo- sag -aa
long- floor.room -be.VII
'it has a long floor area, is a long room'

(41) nibiiw- isag -ad
wet- wood -be.VII
'it (wood) is wet, water-logged'

(42) ginoo- sag -ad
long- useful.wood -be.VII
'it (useful wood) is long'

The fourth medial exhibiting entity (43–44) and quality semantics (45–46) is -*adaawang*- 'sand; sand-like, powder'.

(43) waabishk- adaawang -aa
white- sand -be.VII
'there is white sand'

(44) babiikw- adaawang -aa
bumps- sand -be.VII
'there are sand dunes'

(45) waabishk- adaawang -ad
white- powder -be.VII
'it (sand-like, powder) is white'

(46) biis- adaawang -ad
clean- sand.like -be.VII
'it (sand-like) is fine'

The fifth medial exhibiting entity (47–48) and quality semantics (49–50) is *-jiishkiwag-* 'mud; mud-like (e.g., dough or clay)'.

(47) bengo- jiishkiwag -aa
dry- mud -be.VII
'there is dry mud'

(48) nooki- jiishkiwag -aa
soft- mud -be.VII
'there is soft mud'

(49) bengo- jiishkiwag -ad
dry- mud -be.VII
'it (something mud-like) is dry'

(50) nooki- jiishkiwag -ad
soft- mud.like -be.VII
'it is soft mud, is soft as mud'

The sixth medial exhibiting entity (51–52) and quality semantics (53–54) is -(*a*)*kamig*- 'land, ground, landscape; event'.

(51) maan- akamig -aa
bad- ground -be.VII
'it is poor ground, is rough ground'

(52) in- akamig -aa
in.a.certain.manner- ground -be.VII
'it is ground of a certain slope, condition'

(53) maan- akamig -ad
bad- event -be.VII
'it is an unfortunate or tragic event'

(54) in- akamig -ad
in.a.certain.manner- event -be.VII
'it is a certain event, happens in a certain way'

The last medial, *-bag-* 'leaf', occurs with both VII finals *-aa* (55) and *-ad* (56), but represents a more complicated semantic picture as its entity and quality semantics are usually identically translated. This medial may appear to simply be an incorporated medial with entity semantics that defies our pattern under discussion; however, it may co-occur with an overt noun (57), which is the clearest indicator of classifier status.

(55) misko- bag -aa
red- leaf -be.VII
'there are red leaves'

(56) misko- bag -ad
red- leaf -be.VII
'it has red leaves, is a red leaf'

(57) Banasko- bag -aabaawe -wan waabigwan -iin.
uncoil- leaf -it.is.immersed.vii -IN.PL flower -IN.PL
'The rain makes the flowers open up.'

How can we tease apart the quality semantics from the obvious entity semantics of 'leaf'? It may help to translate the meanings as 'leaf; sheetlike plant matter (leaves, petals, flowers)'.[6] This translation better captures the fact that this medial may classify petals and entire flowers as well as leaves, which we distinguish from each other in nonscientific, everyday English. It should be noted that, to the expert, petals are considered a 'modified leaf', except the petals of certain flowers in the Asteraceae family, such as sunflowers and daisies, which are considered flowers themselves on a composite head (Petruzzello 2023). Understanding that the differences and similarities between leaves, petals, and flowers is nuanced in ways not captured by everyday English may help us to understand that the medial *-bag-* has both the entity meaning 'leaf', as well as a quality meaning that includes an abstraction over that which is shared by entire flowers, petals, and leaves, that is, that they are or are composed of leaves. This particular medial also highlights the second pattern distinguishing VII finals *-aa* and *-ad*, which affects the semantics of entire verbs and is discussed next.

Verbs with VII Final -aa *and Existence Semantics, VII Final* -ad *and Predicative Semantics*

Another pattern found throughout the examples was that between existential semantics in verbs with *-aa* and predicative semantics in verbs with *-ad*. Existential semantics in verbs with *-aa* refer to meanings of 'there is X' or 'there are X', in which X is a combination of the initial and medial meanings and the existence of an entity or entities is asserted. Predicative semantics in verbs with *-ad* refer to meanings of 'it is X' and 'it has X', in which X is again a combination of the initial and medial meanings and an identifying *quality* is asserted. In the following examples, (58), (60), and (62) all occur with *-aa* and have existential semantics. In contrast, (59), (61), and (63) all occur with *-ad* and show predicative semantics.

(58) agaasi- bag -aa
small- leaf -be.VII
'there are small leaves'

(59) agaasi- bag -ad
small- leaf -be.VII
'it is a small leaf'

(60) ozhaashi- jiishkiwag -aa
slippery- mud -be.VII
'there is slippery mud'

(61) ozhaashi- jiishkiwag -ad
slippery- mud -be.VII
'it is slippery mud'

(62) in- aabik -aa
in.a.certain.manner- mineral -be.VII
'there is a certain kind of rock; there is rock or a rocky ridge going a certain way'

(63) in- aabik -ad
in.a.certain.manner- mineral -be.VII
'it (something mineral) is a certain way'

As stated above, verbs with medials and the final *-ad* may also be translated as 'it has X'. These translations are still identifying a single specified object and describing a quality of that object. If anything, the 'it has X' meaning makes it clearer that the verb is predicating some identifying quality, rather than the mere existence of an entity. Examples (65) and (66) are translated as 'it has . . . ', even when the corresponding *-aa* verb in (64) is translated as 'there are . . . '.

(64) misko- bag -aa
red- leaf -be.VII
'there are red leaves'

(65) misko- bag -ad
red- leaf -be.VII
'it has red leaves, is a red leaf'

(66) mich- aakw- ashk -ad
big- stick- plant -be.VII
'it (plant) has a big stalk'

We did find some examples where a verb with the *-aa* final showed predicative semantics, but only in conjunction with existential semantics. That is, verbs with *-aa* always showed existential semantics, but on rare occasions *also* included an optional predicative meaning. For the medial *-ashk-* 'grass, stalk; plant', the *-aa* verb shows both existential *and* predicative meanings (67), while the *-ad* verb only has predicative meanings (68).

(67) nibiiw- ashk -aa
wet- plant -be.VII
'there is wet grass; there are wet stalks, wet plants; it (stalk, plant) is wet'

(68) ishp- ashk -ad
high- plant -be.VII
'it (plant, grass) has a high stalk, is high'

The previous pattern of medials with *-aa* expressing entity semantics and medials with *-ad* expressing quality semantics is related to the pattern of verbs with *-aa* expressing existential semantics and verbs with *-ad* expressing predicative semantics. In verbs with *-aa*, the medial denotes an entity that exists. In verbs with *-ad*, the medial identifies some subject and predicates a quality expressed by the initial.

Effects of Animacy and Further Discussion

Although the patterns reported in this paper are found in inanimate intransitive verbs (VII), those containing the VII final *-ad* often pattern with their animate intransitive verb (VAI) counterparts, for example in verbs with the VAI final -izi 's/he is'. That is, when a verb exists with the three different endings (*-aa*, *-ad*, and *-izi*), *-ad* and *-izi* typically have the same meaning in contrast with *-aa*. In the examples below, the animate verbs and the *-ad* inanimate verbs have quality classifier meanings, while the *-aa* verbs have concrete, entity semantics. The shift in meaning also targets the predicative and existential alternation; while the *-aa* verbs show the existential meaning 'there is X' the other verbs take a predicative meaning, 'it is X'. This pattern is very clear in the examples below, where the *-ad* verbs in (70) and (73) perfectly match their *-izi* counterparts in (71) and (74) with only the difference in animacy. The former showcase predicative meanings with quality semantics, whereas (69) and (72) showcase concrete existential semantics.

(69) waabishk- adaawang -aa
white- sand -be.VII
'there is white sand'

(70) waabishk- adaawang -ad
white- sand -be.VII
'it (sand-like, powder) is white'

(71) waabishk- adaawang -izi
white- sand -be.VAI
's/he, it (sand-like, powder) is white'

(72) bengo- jiishkiwag -aa
dry- mud -be.VII
'there is dry mud'

(73) bengo- jiishkiwag -ad
dry mud be.VII
'it (something mud-like) is dry'

(74) bengo- jiishkiwag -izi
dry- mud -be.VAI
's/he, it (animate; mud-like) is dry'

Denny (1978) offers an analysis of patterns much broader than but pertaining to those discussed here, namely the expression of events, states, and processes as they relate to abstract finals *-aa*, *-ad*, *-in*, and *-e* in Ojibwe and their cognates in other Algonquian languages. We focus our discussion here on the aspects of the proposal related to the finals *-aa* and *-ad*; Denny argues for two types of states based on a spatial versus nonspatial distinction to account for the respective meanings found in verbs with medials and the VII finals *-aa* (spatial) and *-ad* (nonspatial/stative). While we agree with Denny's observations on the importance of the specification of space for defining the patterning of medials with finals *-aa* and *-ad*, we ground our interpretation of this information in crosslinguistic research on classifiers.

Rijkhoff (1991:291, 2010) defines nominal aspect as referring to the linguistic representation of a property in space, similar to how verbal aspect refers to the representation of a property or relation in time. All types of nominal aspect are defined by their specifications or lack thereof for the properties of space and homogeneity, as shown in Table 2.

Singular object nouns correspond to count nouns and are specified for shape but not homogeneity, for example, a bicycle. Sort nouns are found in languages with sortal classifiers, such as Ojibwe (Meyer 2018), and are unspecified for both shape and homogeneity, for example, *biinzikawaagan* 'jacket' in combination with a verb containing the verbal classifier *-iig* 'sheetlike'. Ojibwe also has mass nouns, which are unspecified for shape but are specified as homogeneous, for example, *bezhigwaatig biiwaabik* 'one metal rod' (literally 'one-sticklike metal'). We tentatively suggest that Denny's observation may be integrated here by way of positing the final *-aa* as occurring with meanings of singular object, that is, count, nouns and the final *-ad* as occurring with meanings of sort and mass nouns. This captures Rhodes's (2016:291) observation that many of the medial meanings with *-aa* refer to landforms, as well as the distinction of space made by Denny, since count nouns are specified for shape, while sort and mass nouns are not. Further research is needed to define the relationship between classifiers and predicative versus existential verb meanings.

The Ojibwe language forms shared here raise important questions about our understanding of morpheme identity in Algonquian and other polysynthetic

TABLE 2. Rijkhoff's types of nominal aspect

	- *HOMOGENEITY*	+ *HOMOGENEITY*
- *SHAPE*	General	
	Sort	Mass
+ *SHAPE*	Set	
	Singular Object	Collective

languages, especially with regard to the Algonquian-specific term MEDIAL. Meaning and syntactic environment may be used to determine morpheme identity, that is, whether identical phonological forms should be considered as the same or different morphemes. For example, in English we have *un-* occurring in the verb *unseated* as well as the adjective *unpainted.* In the former, *un-* means that someone was seated and was then removed from the seat, while in the latter, the painting never occurred at all. So, while these meanings of *un-* are certainly related, they are not the same. This, in combination with their differing syntactic environments (verb vs. adjective) leads us to categorize these as two separate morphemes.

Such separation is harder to justify when identical phonological forms have related meanings and occur in the same syntactic environment, as is the case with many medials in Ojibwe. How should we categorize a medial such as *-aabik-* 'rock; mineral (stone, glass, metal)' that shows different but related meanings in the same syntactic environment, that is, verbs, dependent on the verb final *-aa* versus *-ad*? In this situation, we need to also examine the function of the morpheme(s). In a verb with the final *-aa*, *-aabik-* functions as a simple incorporated medial, while in a verb with the final *-ad*, it functions as a verbal classifier, licensing an associated, overt noun. It may be untenable to maintain that *-aabik-* is the same morpheme in verbs with final *-aa* as in verbs with final *-ad* given their distinct functions. Should we, then, continue to refer to these instantiations of *-aabik-* as the same medial?

While this research may complicate our understanding of what constitutes morpheme identity in Algonquian languages and whether the term MEDIAL may encompass separate but related morphemes, it reinforces our understanding of the relationship between medials and certain verb finals. In prior research on Ojibwe, it was shown that the most accurate diagnostics for medials being labeled as classifiers are exhibiting quality semantics and co-occurring with an associated noun (Whitney et al. 2023). Given that co-occurrence of the VII final *-ad* coincides with these characteristics in medials, we find it to be a reliable diagnostic for verbal classifier status.

Similarly, a verb final referred to as incorporating *-e* has also been discussed as a potential diagnostic for incorporated nouns and medials (Wolfart 1973; O'Meara 1990:251; Valentine 2001:412); however, this assertion is controversial for multiple reasons. First, Biedny et al. (2021:38–40) note that this particular final lacks cognates in some Algonquian languages. Second and third, Wolfart (1973:67–68; as cited in Biedny et al. 2021:38) argues that incorporating *-e* is actually optional, and that it is homophonous with a separate Animate Intransitive verb final, which causes confusion. While we do not take a position on the applicability of incorporating *-e* as a diagnostic for incorporation here, it is of interest that verb finals have previously been explored as potential criteria for distinguishing incorporating and classifying medials. Indeed, on the topic of labeling morphemes that precede the VII final *-aa*, Valentine (2001:365) acknowledges that some researchers prefer the label of prefinal instead of medial, because of their proclivity to occur with certain verb finals. He ultimately treats them as medials because they often occur in medial position in nouns, especially with the abstract noun final *-w*, which does not surface when word final. To our knowledge, no one has yet proposed a verb final as a diagnostic for classifier status.

Conclusions and Areas for Further Research

The VII finals *-aa* and *-ad* show systematic and predictable patterns with respect to the semantics of medials and verbs. Namely, occurrence with the final *-aa* is associated with entity semantics of the medial and existential semantics of the entire verb, whereas occurrence with the final *-ad* is associated with quality semantics of the medial and predicative semantics of the entire verb. While many medials occur solely with one or the other verb final and show stable semantics, some medials may occur with both finals and show both entity and quality semantics, depending on the verb final. The shift to quality semantics is also accompanied by a change in syntax, as classifier medials license the use of overt nouns.

Unnoticed, this variability may have caused these medials to be mislabeled as only incorporating or only classificatory. The label MEDIAL may be understood to potentially encompass separate morphemes with identical forms and different, but related, meanings and functions. In their survey of medials across the Algonquian language family, Biedny et al. (2021:41) note, "We have seen parallel cases repeatedly in the classifier data reviewed above," referring to examples where medials appear to have both classifier and nonclassifier instantiations, writing further, "while most Algonquianists treat the distinction between classifiers and incorporated nominals as a binary, in Denny's view a given medial can function as a classifier in one case but be incorporated in another." Biedny et al. argue for a cline of grammaticalization, where a given medial may be fully grammaticalized and function as a classifier, ungrammaticalized and functioning as an incorporated medial, or somewhere in between. Instead of placing medials on a continuum, we argue that they either are or are not classifiers, and some may be both. For those medials that may be both, we highlight two potential analyses: the medial may represent two homophonous morphemes, or it may be polysemous. In the former analysis, what appears to be a single medial behaving both as a classifier and as an incorporated medial would, in fact, be two homophonous medials with different underlying meanings and properties. Under the latter analysis, the polysemous medial would include two different, but related, meanings. Having more knowledge of verb finals and their effect on medial semantics prevents this factor from confounding our growing understanding of medials. We also find *-ad* to be a reliable diagnostic for classifier status of medials in verbs, as it aligns with the previously identified criteria of quality semantics and co-occurring with an overt noun, as shown in Table 3.

Looking toward future research, the present study could be expanded to include more medials and verb finals. Although the medials discussed here represent a broad swath of possible meanings with *-aa* and *-ad*, there are plenty more to be investigated. There is one medial that does not seem to follow the patterns outlined above: *-zigw-* 'icelike, slab; something formed in slabs or cakes; ice'. On semantics alone, this medial appears to have both entity and quality readings, that is, 'ice' and 'icelike' or 'slab' respectively, yet it occurs exclusively with *-aa*.

Further comparison of verb finals that commonly occur with medials, such as *-shin* 's/he falls, lies, treads, contacts, hits on something' or *-sin* 'it falls, lies, contacts, hits on something', could provide additional insights. At least one medial, *-gam-* 'lake; liquid', shows both entity and quality semantics, but not the pattern of occurring with *-aa* for entity semantics and *-ad* for quality semantics. Instead, this medial exhibits entity semantics with *-aa* (75–76) and quality semantics with finals other than *-ad* (77). Interestingly, this is an incorporated medial when occurring with *-aa*, but a classifier medial when expressing quality semantics with other verb finals, evidenced by its ability to co-occur with an overt noun (78). We add

TABLE 3. Table of medial and verbal patterns relating to classifier status

MEDIALS	-*AA*	ENTITY	EXISTENTIAL	PREDICATIVE	QUALITY	-*AD*	OVERT NOUN
-*adin*- 'hill'	+	+	+	-	-	-	-
-*aagonag*- 'snow (on the ground)'	+	+	+	+	-	-	-
-*kob*- 'brush'	+	+	+	+	-	-	-
-(*a*)*kamig*- 'ground; event'	+	+	+	+	+	+	+
-*aabik*- 'rock; mineral'	+	+	+	+	+	+	+
-*aak*(*w*)- 'woods, forest, trees; sticklike, wood'	+	+	+	+	+	+	+
-*adaawang*- 'sand; sand-like, powder'	+	+	+	+	+	+	+
-*bag*- 'leaf'	+	+	+	+	+	+	+
-(*i*)*sag*- 'room, wall, floor; boardlike, wood'	+	+	+	+	+	+	+
-*jiishkiwag*- 'mud; mud-like'	+	+	+	+	+	+	+
-*ashk*- 'grass, stalk; plant	+	+	+	+	+	+	+
-*aad*- 'way of being or life'	-	-	-	+	+	+	+
-*aabiig*- 'stringlike'	-	-	-	+	+	+	+
-*iig*-/-*eg*- 'sheetlike'	-	-	-	+	+	+	+
-*minag*- 'berrylike, small and round'	-	-	-	+	+	+	+
-(*i*)*g*- 'wood, wooden'	-	-	-	+	+	+	+

that, although the dictionary simply lists 'liquid' as one meaning, the translation is closer to 'contained liquid', since all verbs refer to liquid in containers such as pans or kettles. This also aligns well with an abstraction from the incorporated entity semantics of 'lake', which is itself a large body of liquid contained by land.

(75) bitoo- gam -aa
extra.layer- lake -be.VII
'it is a lake parallel to or above another'

(76) aanike- gam -aa
link- lake -be.VII
'it is a chain of lakes'

(77) gizhoo- gam -in
warm- liquid -VII.0.SG
'it (liquid) is warm'

(78) ziigi- gam -izo awe zhiishiibakikoons.
flow.out- liquid -heat.VAI.3 DEM.AN.SG little.tea.kettle
'The tea kettle is boiling over.'

Related to this last point, the potential for issues of dictionary mistranslation necessitates checking this research with fluent speaker intuitions. This would be especially useful in teasing apart the logic of verbal patterning discussed here, as some verbs are translated as having both existential and predicative meanings, despite containing only *-aa* or *-ad.*

NOTES

1. Abbreviations used: 0 = inanimate, 3 = third person, AN = animate noun, DEM = demonstrative, IN = inanimate noun, N = noun, OBV = obviative, POSS = possessive, PST = past tense, PL = plural, SG = singular, VII = inanimate intransitive verb, VAI = animate intransitive verb, VTA = animate transitive verb.
2. While there are other lexical and minor grammatical differences, the Southwestern and Odawa varieties are most noticeably distinct due to syncope, a process of deleting unstressed vowels (Valentine 2001:51–55). As an example, *Anishinaabemowin* is the endonym for the language in the Southwestern dialect, while it is *Nishnaabemwin* in the Eastern and Odawa varieties.
3. We do not discuss the related medial, *-aagon-* 'snow (substance)', as it occurs almost

exclusively with incorporating final *-e*, e.g., *amwaagone* 's/he eats snow'.

4. Example (22) is the only VII with both the medial *-(i)g-* 'wood' and the final *-ad* listed in the *OPD*.
5. The alternation between *-iig-* and *-eg-* 'sheetlike' is phonologically conditioned. Valentine (2001:346, 501) states that *-eg-* surfaces after stems ending in *w*.
6. While 'sheetlike' does not necessarily describe entire flowers, it seems to be the best way to distinguish leaves from other forms of plant matter that are not compatible with this verbal classifier, e.g., stalk or branch.

REFERENCES

Aikhenvald, Alexandra Y. 2000. *Classifiers: A Typology of Noun Categorization Devices*. Oxford: Oxford University Press.

Biedny, Jeremy, Matthew Burner, Andrea Cudworth, and Monica Macaulay. 2021. Classifier Medials across Algonquian: A First Look. *International Journal of American Linguistics* 87(1):1–47.

Bloomfield, Leonard. 1946. Algonquian. *Linguistic Structures of Native America*, ed. by Harry Hoijer, pp. 85–129. Publications in Anthropology 6. New York: Viking Fund.

Denny, J. Peter. 1978. Verb Class Meanings of the Abstract Finals in Ojibway Inanimate Intransitive Verbs. *International Journal of American Linguistics* 44(4):294–322.

Goddard, Ives. 1990. Primary and Secondary Stem Derivation in Algonquian. *International Journal of American Linguistics* 56(4):449–483.

Grinevald, Colette. 2000. A Morphosyntactic Typology of Classifiers. *Systems of Nominal Classification* 4:50–92.

Meyer, Cherry. 2018. Noun Categorization in Ojibwe: Animacy Is Gender and Gender Is Separate from the Count/Mass Distinction. *Papers of the Forty-Seventh Algonquian Conference*, ed. by Margaret Noodin and Monica Macaulay, pp. 199–216. East Lansing: Michigan State University Press.

Meyer, Cherry. 2020. Noun Categorization in Ojibwe: Gender and Classifiers. PhD thesis, University of Chicago.

Mithun, Marianne. 1986. The Convergence of Noun Classification Systems. *Noun Classes and Categorization*, ed. by Colette Craig, pp. 379–397. Amsterdam: John Benjamins.

O'Meara, John. 1990. Delaware Stem Morphology. PhD thesis, McGill University.

Ojibwe People's Dictionary. 2021. Department of American Indian Studies, University of Minnesota. http://ojibwe.lib.umn.edu.

Petruzzello, Melissa. 2023. Petal. *Encyclopedia Britannica*. https://www.britannica.com/

science/petal.

Rhodes, Richard A. 2016. On the Semantics of Abstract Finals: 35 Years Later. *Papers of the Forty-Fourth Algonquian Conference*, ed. by Margaret Noodin, Monica Macaulay, and J. Randolph Valentine, pp. 289–310. Albany: SUNY Press.

Rijkhoff, Jan. 1991. Nominal Aspect. *Journal of Semantics* 8(4):291–309.

Rijkhoff, Jan. 2010. On Flexible and Rigid Nouns. *Parts of Speech: Empirical and Theoretical Advances*, ed. by Umberto Ansaldo, Jan Don, and Roland Pfau, pp. 227–252. Benjamin Current Topics 25. Amsterdam: John Benjamins.

Valentine, J. Randolph. 2001. *Nishnaabemwin Reference Grammar*. Toronto: University of Toronto Press.

Whitney, Anna, Garrett Johnson, and Cherry Meyer. 2023. A Survey of Medials in Ojibwe: Classifiers Versus Incorporation. *Papers of the Fifty-Second Algonquian Conference*, ed. by Margaret Noodin and Monica Macaulay, pp. 361–378. East Lansing: Michigan State University Press.

Wolfart, H. Christoph. 1973. Plains Cree: A Grammatical Study. *Transactions of the American Philosophical Society* 63(5):1–90.

A Computational Model for Blackfoot Demonstratives

Katherine Schmirler, Dominik Kadlec, Inge Genee, and Antti Arppe

In this paper we present a computational model for Blackfoot demonstratives, test its effectiveness, and examine the occurrence of demonstratives in a small corpus of Blackfoot. This demonstrative model complements ongoing development of computational models for verbal and nominal morphology and morphophonology in Blackfoot, whose ultimate objective is to contribute to the development of advanced digital tools in support of Blackfoot language teaching and learning, including an intelligent web-based dictionary, parsers, and spellcheckers (Kadlec 2023; Schmirler et al. 2024).[1]

We begin by briefly reviewing previous work on the structure and function of Blackfoot demonstratives and describing their basic morphology. We then describe how we created and tested our computational model. Next we investigate which of the theoretically hundreds of possible demonstrative forms actually occur in a small corpus of Blackfoot. In the final section we present our conclusions and directions for future work.

Blackfoot Demonstratives

Previous work on Blackfoot demonstratives has largely focused on their semantic and pragmatic functions (Schupbach 2013a,b, 2015; Frantz 2017; Bliss and Wiltschko 2020) and on their syntax (Bliss 2013; Frantz 2017; Windsor 2018; Windsor and Lewis 2018). Our goal here is to more fully investigate the complex morphology of Blackfoot demonstratives by applying computational modeling to investigate the full inventory of possible forms.[2]

Table 1 summarizes the basic morphological structure of Blackfoot demonstratives, as used to build the model described below. The Root and the Inflection are the only obligatory elements within the model; all others are optional.[3] The three basic roots *am, ann, om* distinguish proximal, distal, and remote locations from the speaker as anchor. An optional diminutive suffix occurs rarely "for referents which the speaker views with pathos or affection: generally older persons and children" (Frantz 2017:68). The optional "interior geometric configuration" or "restrictor" suffix *-o* occurs only with the *am* and *ann* stems and restricts the location of the referent to the space shared between speaker and hearer (Schupbach 2013a, 2015; also Taylor 1969:207; Proulx 1988:311–312). Demonstratives are then inflected for person, number, and obviation; the animate singular (proximate) suffix *-wa* does not occur on forms ending with the *-o* restrictor; *-yi* occurs twice in the list because it can mean both inanimate singular or obviative (animate) singular.[4] A series of four

TABLE 1. Structure of Blackfoot demonstratives (adapted from Bliss 2013 and Schupbach 2013a; see also Bliss and Wiltschko 2020; Frantz 2017; Schupbach 2013b, 2015)

ROOT	DIMINUTIVE	RESTRICTOR	INFLECTION	POSTINFLECTIONAL	VERBALIZER
am 'proximal' ann 'distal' om 'remote'	-sst	-o 'interior'	-wa 'proximate singular' -yi 'obviative singular' -yi 'inanimate singular' -iksi 'animate plural' -istsi 'inanimate plural'	-ma 'stationary' -ya 'moving away from speaker' -ka 'moving toward speaker' -hka 'invisible'	-o'ka -ayi
STEM			SUFFIXES		

TABLE 2. Blackfoot demonstrative stems

ROOT ONLY	ROOT+DIMINUTIVE	ROOT+RESTRICTOR	ROOT+DIMINUTIVE+RESTRICTOR
am	amsst	amo	amssto
ann	annsst	anno	annsto
om	omsst		

optional postinflectional suffixes indicate referent/region configuration features relating to motion and visibility (Taylor 1969:201; Schupbach 2013a:60–73; Frantz 2017:72). Finally, a verbalizer, which takes one of two forms, may be added to turn the demonstrative into a copula-like verbal phrase.

The possible combinations of Root, Diminutive, and Restrictor create the set of ten stems given in Table 2. These ten stems can then combine with the obligatory inflectional suffixes and the optional postinflectional and verbalizing suffixes to create a total of 750 distinct forms.[5] The overview given in Tables 1 and 2 ignores pitch accent placement, which can occur on the initial or a noninitial syllable. The accented syllable is usually lengthened, while an unaccented initial syllable is often deleted (Frantz 2017:71–72).[6]

Blackfoot is not the only Algonquian language with a large number of theoretically possible demonstrative forms, but we have not seen numbers quite this high. Junker and MacKenzie (2003) give paradigms for East Cree where, depending on the dialect and depending on how one counts the forms given, there are at least 74 distinct forms (excluding dialect variants) by our count. Plains Cree appears to have about 15 distinct forms (12 with syncretism) (Okimāsis 2018:43, 181).

Morphological Modeling of Blackfoot Demonstratives

In this section we describe the process of creating a morphological model for Blackfoot demonstratives and how the model's effectiveness is tested.

The Model

To model Blackfoot demonstratives, we use a finite-state transducer (FST)–based model (e.g., Beesley and Karttunen 2003), which is well-suited to the relatively straightforward agglutinative morphology, as shown in Table 1. An FST-based morphological model consists of two main components: (1) the `lexc` file(s), which list the possible roots and stems of a language, and the morphemes (arranged into sequences of morphemic slots) with which they can combine to create words, and (2) the `xfscript` file, which gives morphophonological rules. These consist of underlying and surface representations. The underlying side consists of the stems plus tags to represent relevant grammatical information (e.g., `+Dem` for demonstrative), as well as tags to represent the grammatical features of any additional morphemes. The surface side shows the exponence of these features (e.g., the stem *am-*, the suffix *-wa* for animate singular). The surface forms here are not the true surface forms, but rather the input to the morphophonological rules, which are given as rewrite rules in the `xfscript` formalism (e.g., Kadlec 2023; Schmirler et al. 2024). The `xfscript` rules are then applied to the output of the `lexc` to generate wordforms. As a finite-state transducer, the model can also work in reverse, analyzing surface forms and returning underlying tag representations. It is this latter functionality that is the focus of the present work. When working with corpus data from sources using slightly different spelling conventions, one further component is needed—an orthographical relaxer, which allows for spelling variation in surface forms. For example, we allow for variation in vowel length and accent, variation in the length of geminate consonants, and short unstressed vowel deletion.

For the current work, the model is compiled using the foma finite-state compiler (Hulden 2009), which is one of the open-source implementations for compiling Xerox-style finite-state models (Beesley and Karttunen 2003). A finite-state compiler allows for the underlying code, the `lexc` and `xfscript` files, to be readily transformed into finite-state machines that can analyze and generate words, with possible extensions to numerous other functionalities.

To create a demonstrative model for Blackfoot, we use the `lexc` formalism to build up the morpheme concatenation, essentially following the morphological template given in Table 1. However, to simplify the modeling process, we "chunk" the stem morphology into its possible permutations (as in Table 2) and dynamically model only the suffixes (for more on chunking when modeling an Algonquian language, see Harrigan et al. 2017). As this model is fairly compact, we present the morpheme concatenation here in its entirety.[7] The stems are set up as in (1). The `LEXICON` label represents a morphological slot in the template, here the demonstrative stems. The material before the colon is the underlying form, giving the stem plus tags.[8] Following the colon is the surface form to which the suffixes attach. Finally, after the surface forms, the model is directed to the next morpheme slot in the template, which gives the suffixes for animacy and number. This slot is given in (2).

(1) Demonstrative stems in the `lexc` file[9]

```
LEXICON Dem
am+Dem:am Dem_num_suffixes ;
am+Dem+Dim:amsst Dem_num_suffixes ;
amo+Dem:amo Dem_num_suffixes ;
amo+Dem+Dim:amssto Dem_num_suffixes ;
ann+Dem:ann Dem_num_suffixes ;
ann+Dem+Dim:annst Dem_num_suffixes ;
anno+Dem:anno Dem_num_suffixes ;
anno+Dem+Dim:annssto Dem_num_suffixes ;
om+Dem:om Dem_num_suffixes ;
om+Dem+Dim:omsst Dem_num_suffixes ;
```

(2) Animacy and number suffixes

```
LEXICON Dem_num_suffixes
+A+Sg:%>^DEMwa Dem_postinfl ;
+A+Obv:%>yi Dem_postinfl ;
+I+Sg:%>yi Dem_postinfl ;
+A+Pl:%>^DEMiksi Dem_postinfl ;
+I+Pl:%>^DEMistsi Dem_postinfl ;
```

In (2), we see that the underlying side now no longer includes a stem, but just the tags for the features of the suffixes added on the surface side, which are marked as suffixes and delineated by the suffix boundary marker `%>`. We also have the inclusion of the trigger `^DEM`, which is used by the morphophonological rules in two ways. First, the rules fully delete the suffix *-wa* after demonstrative stems ending in *-o* (Frantz 2017:69–70); the verbal third person singular suffix is also *-wa*, but does not delete in this phonological context, so the trigger marks a morphological context instead.[10] Similarly, the trigger is used for the plural suffixes, though in this case, the deletion affects only the initial vowel *i*, and is optional (i.e., *amoiksi* and *amoksi* are both generated). The model is then directed to the next slot for postinflectional suffixes as in (3).

(3) Postinflectional suffixes

```
LEXICON Dem_postinfl
+Stat:%>ma Vblz ;
+Movg:%>ya Vblz ;
+Invs:%>hka Vblz ;
+MT:%>ka Vblz ;
0 Vblz ;
```

In this slot, we now have the option of a `0`, which indicates that no suffix is required to be added in this section. Alternatively, one could use just the label name `Vblz` to achieve the same end and move to the next lexicon, but we have opted to make this empty slot explicit. The model moves to the next and final slot, for the verbalizing suffixes in (4).

(4) Verbalizing suffixes

```
LEXICON Vblz
+Vblz:%>o'ka # ;
+Vblz:%>ayi # ;
0 # ;
```

There are two possible verbalizing suffixes, which are for now given the same tag. After these suffixes are added, the pound sign # indicates that the word ends (i.e., that there is no further morpheme slot). Again, we have a `0` option, that is, verbalizing suffixes are optional. Thus, a demonstrative only requires a stem and an animacy/number suffix, with optional postinflectional and verbalizing suffixes.

Finally, the output here is transformed by the morphophonological rules. The existing rules (e.g., Kadlec 2023; Schmirler et al. 2024) created for modeling nouns and verbs required essentially no additions for the demonstratives, with the exception of accounting for the `^DEM` trigger and the deletion of *-wa* and optionally *i* after *-o*. Additionally, some extra changes were required in the spelling relaxer, allowing both *a* and *o* to delete word-initially and some further vowel accent variation. Note that the freedom allowed by the relaxer means that some ambiguity is allowed for; for example, *ma* can be either *ama* or *oma*.

Testing the Model

The model testing process has two main components. First, we test how well the model applies to standardized forms (without the relaxer), which is done through so-called YAML files. Second, we test how well the model applies to forms in a corpus, which can occur with variation including accent placement, vowel deletion, and length variation.[11]

YAML files present a series of underlying and surface representations, with the goal of representing the different possible patterns to ensure that the morphological and morphophonological rules are working as intended. For our testing purposes, we created files for the stems *am-*, *anno-* and *omsst-*, which cover the different stem possibilities (Table 2). An example of the underlying/surface pairs for *am-* are given in (5). These test sets were created in tandem with the model by Schmirler, using Table 1 as a guide, as a full list of demonstrative forms did not exist to our knowledge, and the tagging needed to be consistent between the model and the YAML files. Without access to the model, the test forms were independently verified by Genee.

(5) Examples from YAML file for *am*

```
am+Dem+A+Sg: ama
am+Dem+I+Sg: ami
am+Dem+A+Obv: ami
am+Dem+A+Pl: amiksi
am+Dem+I+Pl: amistsi
am+Dem+A+Sg+Stat: amama
am+Dem+I+Sg+Stat: amima
am+Dem+A+Obv+Stat: amima
am+Dem+A+Pl+Stat: amiksima
am+Dem+I+Pl+Stat: amistsima
am+Dem+A+Sg+Movg: amaya
am+Dem+I+Sg+Movg: amiya
am+Dem+A+Obv+Movg: amiya
am+Dem+A+Pl+Movg: amiksiya
am+Dem+I+Pl+Movg: amistsiya
```

Though further confirmation of all the standardized forms with native speakers is a goal for the future, the current YAML files and morphological model return a 100% generation and recognition for all demonstrative forms.

The next step of testing allows us to see how well the model performs with the corpus, where many forms display some sort of variation from what the YAML files represent, including vowel accents, vowel deletion, and length variation using the relaxer. While the effectiveness here cannot be evaluated as neatly as with YAMLs, we observe that very few apparent demonstratives remain unrecognized in the corpus. Those that are unrecognized are due to two main issues for future model development: (1) as-yet-unmodeled morphology, such as interrogative suffixes or contractions of *ki* plus a demonstrative, and (2) cases of more complex deletion or accent placement, where decisions remain to be made if these are to be dealt with in the morphophonological rules or the relaxer or, if they are very frequent, hard-coded in the morphotax.[12]

Examining Demonstratives in a Corpus

The demonstrative system of Blackfoot is considerably more extensive than that of most other Algonquian languages, with 750 theoretically possible forms according to our calculations. Through a small corpus exploration we investigate which of the theoretically possible stem and suffix types occur in texts and in what combinations and which morphemes occur most frequently.

The corpus used in this study is that compiled by Kadlec (2023) for building and evaluating the verb and noun computational models for Blackfoot. This corpus adheres to the orthography laid out by Frantz (2017), whose work also heavily underlies the morphological and morphophonological models for Blackfoot described in Kadlec (2023), Schmirler et al. (2024), and herein. The texts are collected from several sources, including (1) examples or stories from Frantz's (2017) Blackfoot grammar, (2) examples from Frantz and Russell's (2017) Blackfoot dictionary (dataset compiled by Weber 2022; see Weber et al. 2023), (3) Siksika translations of the Jehovah's Witness website (https://www.jw.org/en/library/?contentLanguageFilter=bla), (4) Blackfoot translations of the Glenbow Museum website (https://www.glenbow.org/blackfoot/BL/html/index.htm), (5) transcribed stories from the online Blackfoot dictionary website (https://stories.blackfoot.atlas-ling.ca/#/stories), (6) transcribed words and phrases from the online Blackfoot dictionary website (https://blackfoot.algonquianlanguages.ca/conversations/), and (7) stories from the book *Ákaitsinikssistsi: Blackfoot Stories of Old* (Russell and Genee 2014).

TABLE 3. Demonstrative types and tokens in a Blackfoot corpus

	CORPUS	DEMONSTRATIVES	% OF CORPUS
Types	13,582	207	1.52%
Tokens	16,733	990	5.92%
TTR	0.81	0.21	

The corpus is analyzed using the above-described model for demonstratives, with the nominal and verbal models set aside. A visual examination of the analyzed corpus has noted a small number of unanalyzed demonstratives, though a full report of accuracy is beyond the scope of the present work.[13] The type and token counts for the full corpus and demonstratives within the corpus as recognized by the model, with spelling relaxation, are given in Table 3. The full corpus counts include some limited English words and numerals, though punctuation has been removed for this table.

The counts for demonstratives reported in Table 3 include all unique surface forms in the corpus, with whatever vowel length variation, accent variation, or deletion that occurs resulting in different forms regardless of their morphological similarities. If we ignore this variation and look only at the morphological tags, 81 of the possible 750 demonstrative tag sequences produced by the model occur in the corpus (10.8%), or 63 unique surface forms (10.5% of 600 possible forms, with syncretism between the animate obviative and inanimate singular forms).[14] Focusing on the surface forms, we can then compare these 63 forms to the 207 types in the corpus: ignoring the variation reduces these by over two thirds.

Next, we explore the ambiguity of forms in the corpus. We identify two main types of ambiguity here: (1) inherent ambiguity, for example, syncretism between obviative and inanimate suffixes, and (2) ambiguity introduced by vowel deletion/shortening. This includes forms with initial vowel deletion like *ma*, which receives analyses for both *am-* and *om-*, those with final vowel deletion like *om*, which receives analyses for animate singular, inanimate singular, and animate obviative, and length variation, like *annayi*, which is the surface form for inanimate/obviative singular *ann-* plus the verbalizer *-ayi*, but also a reduced form of *annaayi*, the same form for animate singular. Counts for these are given in Table 4.

Next, we explore the counts for different morphemes, not accounting for variation (Tables 5–8). We exclude here the 45 ambiguous forms that are ambiguous

TABLE 4. Demonstrative ambiguity

	INANIMATE/OBVIATIVE	OTHER AMBIGUITY
Types	67	16
Tokens	437	45
TTR	0.15	0.36

due to vowel deletion/shortening, but include those that are inherently ambiguous. Table 5 looks at the stems, Table 6 at the person/number suffixes, Table 7 at the postinflectional suffixes, and Table 8 at the verbalizers. These tables also include totals; a demonstrative requires a stem and a person/number suffix, so in the first two tables, these are the total of forms without variation, while the totals in the last two tables indicate in how many demonstrative forms these categories are present.

Of these, the most common stem is thus the medial stem *ann*, followed by *amo, am, om,* and *anno*. Diminutives are rare, occurring in five tokens (four types). Singular person/number suffixes occur much more frequently than plural. The most common postinflectional suffix is *-hka* 'invisible'. Of the verbalizing suffixes, *-ayi* is more common than *-o'ka*.

The most common combinations of tags (occurring at least ten times in the corpus) are given in Table 9. For the most part, variation is collapsed and the form

TABLE 5. Occurrence of demonstrative stems

STEM	TYPES	% DEM TYPES	TOKENS	% DEM TOKENS	TTR
am	9	14.3%	80	8.7%	0.11
amsst	1	1.6%	1	0.1%	1.00
amo	15	23.8%	149	16.3%	0.10
amssto	1	1.6%	1	0.1%	1.00
ann	22	34.9%	440	48.0%	0.05
annst	0	0.0%	0	0.0%	0
anno	5	7.9%	50	5.5%	0.10
annsto	1	1.6%	2	0.2%	0.50
om	8	12.7%	192	21.0%	0.04
omsst	1	1.6%	1	0.1%	1.00
Total demonstratives	63		916		0.07

TABLE 6. Occurrence of person and number suffixes

PERSON AND NUMBER	TYPES	% DEM TYPES	TOKENS	% DEM TOKENS	TTR
-wa (A+Sg)	27	42.9%	336	36.7%	0.08
-yi (A+Obv AND I+Sg)	18	28.6%	408	44.5%	0.04
-iksi (A+Pl)	11	17.5%	83	9.1%	0.13
-istsi (I+Pl)	7	11.1%	89	9.7%	0.08
Total demonstratives	63		916		0.07

TABLE 7. Occurrence of postinflectional suffixes

POSTINFLECTIONAL	TYPES	% DEM TYPES	TOKENS	% DEM TOKENS	TTR
-ma (+Stat)	8	12.7%	32	3.5%	0.25
-ya (+Movg)	7	11.1%	11	1.2%	0.64
-ka (+MT)	5	7.9%	20	2.2%	0.25
-hka (+Invs)	17	27.0%	107	11.7%	0.16
Total postinflectional	37	58.7%	170	18.6%	0.22

TABLE 8. Occurrence of verbalizing suffixes

VERBALIZER	TYPES	% DEM TYPES	TOKENS	% DEM TOKENS	TTR
-o'ka (+Vblz)	4	6.3%	23	2.5%	0.17
-ayi (+Vblz)	14	22.2%	34	3.7%	0.41
Total verbalizers	18	28.6%	57	6.2%	0.32

given in the second column is the standard spelling (e.g., *anni* for ann+Dem+I+Sg also surfaced as *anní, ánni, ni, anníí,* etc.). The exceptions here are *mi, ma,* and *miksi,* which can be either *om-* or *am-*; this ambiguity is frequent enough to retain for this particular exploration. Here, we see that the most common combinations are of stems and singular person/number suffixes, then plural suffixes (also suggested by Tables 5 and 6). Where postinflectional suffixes begin to occur, *-hka* 'invisible' (by far the most frequent per Table 7) combines most often with *ann-*; this is unsurprising given that each is the most common in its templatic position, and that the combination *annohka* is frequently used adverbially with the meaning 'now'. Where the limited verbalizers occur, each of these tag sequences surfaced most often as either *-o'ka* or *-ayi*, not both (i.e., am+Dem+A+Sg+Vblz only surfaces in the corpus as

TABLE 9. Most frequent demonstratives in the corpus

TOTAL	STANDARDIZED FORM	ANALYSES
192	*anni*	ann+Dem+I+Sg ann+Dem+A+Obv
91	*anna*	ann+Dem+A+Sg
78	*omi*	om+Dem+I+Sg om+Dem+A+Obv
53	*oma*	om+Dem+A+Sg
50	*amo*	amo+Dem+A+Sg
48	*annistsi*	ann+Dem+I+Pl
40	*amoyi*	amo+Dem+I+Sg amo+Dem+A+Obv
33	*omiksi*	om+Dem+A+Pl
31	*ami*	am+Dem+I+Sg am+Dem+A+Obv
28	*annohka*	anno+Dem+A+Sg+Invs
27	*mi*	om+Dem+I+Sg om+Dem+A+Obv am+Dem+I+Sg am+Dem+A+Obv
26	*anniksi*	ann+Dem+A+Pl
22	*annahka*	ann+Dem+A+Sg+Invs
20	*amao'ka*	am+Dem+A+Sg+Vblz
18	*omistsi*	om+Dem+I+Pl
15	*ma*	om+Dem+A+Sg am+Dem+A+Sg
15	*annihka*	ann+Dem+I+Sg+Invs ann+Dem+A+Obv+Invs
14	*amoistsi*	amo+Dem+I+Pl
14	*ama*	am+Dem+A+Sg
13	*amohka*	amo+Dem+A+Sg+Invs
13	*amoiksi*	amo+Dem+A+Pl
11	*anno*	anno+Dem+A+Sg
11	*annimayi*	ann+Dem+I+Sg+Stat+Vblz ann+Dem+A+Obv+Stat+Vblz
10	*miksi*	om+Dem+A+Pl am+Dem+A+Pl

amao'ka, not *amaayi*, and `ann+Dem+A/I+Obv/Sg+Stat+Vblz` surfaced only as *annimayi*, not *annimao'ka*. There is only one case in the corpus where both possible verbalizers surface for the same tag string, given in (6). Whether such cases are equally rare in a larger corpus and to what extent the morphological or syntactic contexts condition the different verbalizing suffixes are possible questions for future research. Additionally, though *-ayi* is overall the most common verbalizer, *amao'ka* is the most common verbalized demonstrative type.

(6) Verbalizing suffixes
annahkao'k `ann+Dem+A+Sg+Invs+Vblz` (standard: *annahko'ka*)
annááhkayi `ann+Dem+A+Sg+Invs+Vblz` (standard: *annahkaayi*)
'that (animate, not currently visible) is . . . '

Discussion/Conclusion

In our exploration of demonstratives in a corpus of Blackfoot, we were struck by two main phenomena: first, the relatively small number of possible forms that occur, and second, the considerable variation within those that do occur. In this section, we briefly discuss these phenomena, followed by a brief discussion of directions for future model development and research questions.

The computational modeling of Blackfoot demonstratives results in a total of 750 possible tag sequences (representing 600 surface forms), though in the (relatively small) corpus of Blackfoot, only 11% of these possible forms actually occur. This can largely be attributed to the frequency of forms that occur without postinflectional or verbalizing suffixes, as the majority of forms in the corpus occur with only the required stem and person/number suffix. Future research would be needed to determine any patterns to the use of postinflectional and verbalizing suffixes beyond the frequencies reported here. Of the 990 demonstratives that occur in the corpus, roughly half are based on the root *ann-* (i.e., stems *ann-*, *anno-*, and *annsto-*). This is perhaps not surprising given that *ann-* is arguably the most semantically neutral demonstrative available: it designates the middle distance in a three-distance deictic system and does not include any additional elements such as diminutives, restrictors, or postinflectional suffixes. One might even argue that bare *ann-*, only followed by the required inflectional suffix, is the form that comes closest to a definite article in a language without articles. This ubiquity of *ann-* also carries over into the English spoken by Blackfoot speakers. Fluent speakers of Blackfoot, when speaking English, frequently use *annaahka* (usually shortened to *naahk*) followed by a name when discussing a person not present in the conversation, usually with a recognitional function (e.g., "NAAHK Eugene, he speaks fluent Blackfoot").

The shortened version *naahk* for *annaahka* also illustrates a frequent variation that occurs, namely deleted unstressed initial and final vowels. When this kind of variation is ignored, along with accent differences, we see only 63 unique demonstratives in the corpus—just 30% of the 207 unique types including variation. Such variation is also something speakers are aware of, and "shortening" or "abbreviation" of words, especially by younger and less fluent speakers, is often discussed (e.g., "For example ANNÁ, a lot of people just say NAA").

In the future, we plan to pursue a number of paths related to further model development and the investigation of research questions. The development of the computational model is an ongoing project. The morphological model of the demonstratives will be refined, for example allowing for contraction with preceding *ki* 'and', and interrogative suffixes. The demonstrative model then needs to be integrated with the (already partially existing) noun and verb components. Subsequently, pronouns and particles need to be modeled. The resulting computational model, in whole or in part, can be integrated into the online dictionary for improved searches and for generated paradigms.[15]

The testing and development of the model can also go along with corpus expansion and development: with more data to test against, the model can improve, and with more data, further research can be better informed. Some research questions we find of immediate interest include an exploration of the combinations of morphemes within demonstratives, such as with what stems and person suffixes postinflectional and verbalizing suffixes occur, and, for the verbalizing suffixes, which suffix surfaces in which contexts. We can also explore the surface variation, such as where deletion or accent changes happen in context.

Beyond morphology, the syntactic patterns of demonstratives can also be explored using an analyzed corpus, particularly with the addition of a syntactic model to identify which demonstratives are associated with adjacent nouns and which are not, whether a demonstrative specifies a nominal argument or is itself an argument, and so forth. Syntactic modeling allows for not only the identification of syntactic roles, but also for at least some disambiguation of ambiguous forms; for example, an ambiguous inanimate/obviative demonstrative, adjacent to an inanimate or obviative noun, could be identified appropriately. This would then allow for more meaningful statistics when discussing these categories. In developing a syntactic model for Blackfoot, we might also explore how well a model for a related language can be adapted to another, and how the development time changes if one is not starting from scratch. A syntactic model using the Constraint Grammar formalism has been constructed for Plains Cree (e.g., Schmirler et al. 2018; Schmirler 2022); we have yet to assess syntactic similarities and differences between the languages, but the relationship between nouns and demonstratives is an excellent place to start this type of comparative project.

The computational model for Blackfoot demonstratives described here represents only a small piece of the tools needed to model Blackfoot grammar for corpus analysis, lexicography, and other computational tools. However, even just this one component allows us to scratch the surface of a corpus of Blackfoot and examine the (in)frequency of demonstrative forms, and the various spellings they can take, within Blackfoot texts. As the modeling continues, we will come closer to a fully morphologically analyzed corpus of Blackfoot and a deeper understanding of how the language is used.

NOTES

1. This work is supported by SSHRC grants 895-2019-1012 (Partnership Grant to Arppe), 435-2021-0562 (Insight Grant to Genee), and 756-2022-0428 (Postdoctoral Fellowship to Schmirler). Contributor roles: Schmirler: writing, funding, model development; Kadlec: model development, data curation; Genee: funding, writing, model development, bibliography; Arppe: funding, model development, review. Abbreviations used: A = animate; Dem = demonstrative; Dim = diminutive; I = inanimate; Invs = invisible; MT = motion toward; Movg = moving; Obv = obviative; Pl = plural; Sg = singular; Stat = stationary; TTR = type-token ratio; Vblz = verbalizer. Throughout, a monospaced font is used to indicate elements of code.
2. We use the term DEMONSTRATIVES to refer to both demonstrative pronouns and demonstrative determiners. The disambiguation of these will be left to a future syntactic model.
3. Bliss (2013:139) notes that bare stems are possible, though rare. For our current purposes, the model focuses on regular morphology, with rarer cases left to future development.
4. We keep these syncretic forms distinct to simplify syntactic modeling, though we are not yet at this stage of model development.

5. Bliss's (2013:138) count of 900 is probably due to the failure to exclude *om+o* forms from the calculation.
6. Several combinations of a particular root with a particular postinflectional suffix have lexicalized meanings, including *annooma* 'around here', *annohka* 'now', *annama* 'the late (deceased) . . . ', *anniihka* 'before' (Frantz 2017:73).
7. For closed classes such as demonstratives, it is not unreasonable to just list all the possible forms with their tag sequences, rather than modeling the suffix morphology. However, the type of modeling we demonstrate here allows for straightforward marking of the morpheme boundaries and makes the constituent morphemes explicit, which may facilitate the modeling of variation (e.g., where the variation is associated with a particular morpheme).
8. Note that these stems need not be those that might be described in, e.g., a grammar of the language; rather we aim to make the output of the tags more readable. Thus, we separate the forms with and without *-o* in the underlying forms, but add the diminutives through the tag `+Dim` and only show the *-sst* suffix on the surface side, not the underlying.
9. Usually, one uses lemmas to connect the various inflected word forms, and that lemma is what links the various inflected forms to a dictionary entry, as matching the entry heading. However, as the Blackfoot dictionary (Frantz and Russell 2017) is "of stems, roots, and affixes," the stems not only make the modeling more straightforward but also better match the existing dictionary entries.
10. This approach is not a claim as to the structure of Blackfoot, i.e., that *amo* is underlyingly *amo-wa*, but simply allows for symmetry and simplicity in the model.
11. Lexc file: https://github.com/giellalt/lang-bla/blob/main/src/fst/morphology/incoming/dem.lexc; morphophonological rule file: https://github.com/giellalt/lang-bla/blob/main/src/fst/morphology/phonology.xfscript; YAML files: https://github.com/giellalt/lang-bla/tree/main/src/fst/test; spelling relaxer: https://github.com/giellalt/lang-bla/blob/main/src/fst/morphology/incoming/relaxer.regex.
12. We have examined the forms in the corpus and their analyses (or lack thereof), at least for forms that occur more than once in the corpus, and found these patterns for missed demonstratives. For forms that receive ambiguous analyses with spelling relaxation implemented (i.e., analyses for a demonstrative and another part of speech), an examination of these forms finds that the forms are in these cases all demonstratives and the noun or verb analyses arise only due to extensive changes allowed by the relaxer.
13. We must thus acknowledge that the numbers in this section must be taken with a grain of salt; however, given the corpus size and our visual examination of the results, we are

reasonably confident that the overall trends reported here would not be greatly altered by more rigorous validation of the recognition of demonstratives by the model.

14. Compare this with Cyr (1993), who found only eight distinct forms in a small (~2,500 words) corpus of Plains Cree.
15. https://dictionary.blackfoot.algonquianlanguages.ca.

REFERENCES

Beesley, Kenneth R., and Lauri Karttunen. 2003. *Finite-State Morphology*. CSLI Studies in Computational Linguistics. Chicago: University of Chicago Press.

Bliss, Heather. 2013. The Blackfoot Configurationality Conspiracy: Parallels and Differences in Clausal and Nominal Structures. PhD thesis, University of British Columbia.

Bliss, Heather, and Martina Wiltschko. 2020. *Stsíkiistsi ki stsíkiistsi*: The Ubiquity of Blackfoot Demonstratives in Discourse. *Demonstratives in Discourse*, ed. by Åshild Næss, Anna Margetts, and Yvonne Treis, pp. 123–147. Berlin: Language Science Press.

Cyr, Danielle. 1993. Demonstratives and Definite Articles in Plains Cree. *Papers of the Twenty-Fourth Algonquian Conference*, ed. by William Cowan, pp. 64–80. Ottawa: Carleton University.

Frantz, Donald G. 2017. *Blackfoot Grammar*. 3rd ed. Toronto: University of Toronto Press.

Frantz, Donald G., and Norma Jean Russell. 2017. *Blackfoot Dictionary of Stems, Roots, and Affixes*. Toronto: Toronto University Press.

Harrigan, Atticus G., Katherine Schmirler, Antti Arppe, Lene Antonsen, Trond Trosterud, and Arok Wolvengrey. 2017. Learning from the Computational Modelling of Plains Cree Verbs. *Morphology* 27(4):565–598. https://doi.org/10.1007/s11525-017-9315-x.

Hulden, Mans. 2009. Foma: A Finite-State Compiler and Library. *Proceedings of the Demonstrations Session at EACL 2009*, ed. by Jörn Kreutel, pp. 29–32. Athens: Association for Computational Linguistics.

Junker, Marie-Odile, and Marguerite MacKenzie. 2003. Demonstratives in East Cree. *Papers of the Thirty-Fourth Algonquian Conference*, ed. by H. C. Wolfart, pp. 201–215. Winnipeg: University of Manitoba.

Kadlec, Dominik. 2023. A Computational Model of Blackfoot Noun and Verb Morphology. MA thesis, Iniskim University of Lethbridge. https://hdl.handle.net/10133/6635.

Okimāsis, Jean L. 2018. *Cree: Language of the Plains / nêhiyawêwin: paskwâwi-pîkiskwêwin*. Regina: University of Regina Press.

Proulx, Paul. 1988. The Demonstrative Pronouns of Proto-Algonquian. *International Journal of American Linguistics* 54(3):309–330.

Russell, Lena Heavy Shields, and Inge Genee. 2014. *Ákaitsinikssiistsi: Blackfoot Stories of Old.* Regina: University of Regina Press.

Schmirler, Katherine. 2022. Syntactic Features and Text Types in 20th Century Plains Cree: A Constraint Grammar Approach. PhD thesis, University of Alberta. https://doi.org/10.7939/r3-pz87-ye25.

Schmirler, Katherine, Antti Arppe, and Inge Genee. 2024. Morphophonological Rule Development and Real-time Rule Testing with XFST: A Model for Blackfoot. *Papers of the Fifty-Third Algonquian Conference*, ed. by Inge Genee, Monica Macaulay, and Margaret Noodin, pp. 253–268. East Lansing: Michigan State University Press.

Schmirler, Katherine, Antti Arppe, Trond Trosterud, and Lene Antonsen. 2018. Building a Constraint Grammar Parser for Plains Cree Verbs and Arguments. *Proceedings of the Eleventh International Conference on Language Resources and Evaluation (LREC 2018)*, ed. by Nicoletta Calzolari, Khalid Choukri, Christopher Cieri, Thierry Declerck, Sara Goggi, Koiti Hasida, Hitoshi Isahara, Bente Maegaard, Joseph Mariani, Hélène Mazo, Asuncion Moreno, Jan Odijk, Stelios Piperidis, and Takenobu Tokunaga, pp. 2981–2988. Istanbul: European Language Resources Association (ELRA). https://aclanthology.org/L18-1472/.

Schupbach, Shannon Scott. 2013a. The Blackfoot Demonstrative System: Function, Form, and Meaning. MA thesis, University of Montana. https://scholarworks.umt.edu/etd/964/.

Schupbach, Shannon Scott. 2013b. Situational Demonstratives in Blackfoot. *Coyote Papers* 21:1–21. https://repository.arizona.edu/handle/10150/270993.

Schupbach, Shannon Scott. 2015. Blackfoot Demonstratives in Narrative Discourse: A Pragmatic Analysis. *Proceedings of the 10th High Desert Linguistics Conference (2012)*, ed. by Benjamin Anible, Keiko Beers, Laura Hirrel, and Deborah Wager, pp. 131–141. Albuquerque: University of New Mexico Department of Linguistics.

Taylor, Allan R. 1969. A Grammar of Blackfoot. PhD thesis, University of California Berkeley. https://escholarship.org/uc/item/1nx6d3n1.

Weber, Natalie. 2022. Blackfoot Words. https://www.blackfootwords.com/.

Weber, Natalie, Tyler Brown, Joshua Celli, McKenzie Denham, Hailey Dykstra, Rodrigo Hernandez-Merlin, Evan Hochstein, Pinyu Hwang, Nico Kidd, Diana Kulmizev, Hannah Morrison, Matty Norris, and Lena Venkatramann. 2023. Blackfoot Words: A Database of Blackfoot Lexical Forms. *Language Resources and Evaluation* 57:1207–1262. https://doi.org/10.1007/s10579-022-09631-2.

Windsor, Joseph W. 2018. Blackfoot Demonstratives, Referentiality, and Association with the Syntactic Spine. *Proceedings of the Workshop on Structure and Constituency of Languages in the Americas 21, University of British Columbia Working Papers in Linguistics 46*, ed. by Megan Keough, Natalie Weber, Andrei Anghelescu, Sihwie Chen, Erin Guntly, Khia

Johnson, Daniel Reisinger, and Oksana Tkachman, pp. 281–295. Vancouver: University of British Columbia.

Windsor, Joseph W., and Blake Lewis. 2018. Constituency of Demonstratives in Blackfoot: Evidence from Phonology, Syntax and Semantics. *Proceedings of the Workshop on Structure and Constituency of Languages of the Americas 21, University of British Columbia Working Papers in Linguistics 46*, ed. by Megan Keough, Natalie Weber, Andrei Anghelescu, Sihwei Chen, Erin Guntly, Khia Johnson, Daniel Reisinger, and Oksana Tkachman, pp. 297–310. Vancouver: University of British Columbia.

Refining the Phonological Analysis of Ojibwe Nominal Inflection Classes

Reed Steiner and Christopher Hammerly

One well-known property of morphology is ALLOMORPHY: that the particular surface realization of a single morpheme can differ depending on the surrounding morphophonological context. For example, the English regular plural marker alternates between [s], [z], and [ɪz] depending on phonological properties of the stem to which it attaches. One major project in linguistics is to provide the most general account possible of these types of alternations, usually in the form of independently motivated rules or constraints that transform some underlying representation into the form that appears on the surface. The goal of this paper is to advance a general account of the allomorphy present within nominal inflection in Ojibwe (Central Algonquian)—in particular the variety known as Southwestern Ojibwe, spoken in what is now Minnesota, Wisconsin, North Dakota, and parts of Northwestern Ontario.

Nouns can be inflected with morphemes encoding a wide variety of different functions, including markers for person, possession, plurality, location, diminutive, pejorative, possession, and obviation as exemplified in (1) (Nichols 2011; *Ojibwe People's Dictionary* 2021).

(1) a. ni-jiimaan-**inaan** 'our boat' person (PER)
b. ni-zhiishiib-**im** 'my duck' possessive (POSS)
c. aninishib-**ag** 'mallards' animate plural (PL.ANIM)
d. abwaan-**an** 'roasts' inanimate plural (PL.INAN)
e. ishkode-**ng** 'in, at, to the fire' locative (LOC)
f. jiimaan-**ens** 'small boat' diminutive (DIM)
g. odaaban-**ish** 'no-good car' pejorative (PEJ)
h. noos-**iban** 'my late father' preterit (PRET)
i. ikwew-**an** 'woman' obviative (OBV)

This paper is not focused on the meaning or use of these morphemes (for a general overview, see Valentine 2001), but rather mapping and understanding the various forms that they can take. For illustrative purposes, let us temporarily set aside the fact that the addition of pieces of morphology might in fact condition changes to the stem rather than the stem giving rise to a change in the morpheme, and consider the surface range of the animate plural morpheme, as exemplified in (2). We see that plural marking on animate nouns is associated with no less than six different surface forms (*-ag*, *-yag*, *-g*, *-wag*, *-oog*, *-iig*), which are only united by the shared presence of the segment /g/.

(2) a. zhiishiib 'duck' + [plural] = zhiishii**bag**
b. giigoonh 'fish' + [plural] = giigoon**hyag**
c. anishinaabe 'Ojibwe' + [plural] = anishinaab**eg**
d. inini 'man' + [plural] = inini**wag**
e. mitig 'tree' + [plural] = miti**goog**
f. asin 'stone' + [plural] = asin**iig**

The realization of different forms has led to the descriptive project of sorting nouns into *classes* based on shared inflectional patterns (e.g., Nichols 1980; Valentine 2001; Nichols 2011). For example, nouns where the animate plural marker appears as *-oog* (2e) are sorted into class 4a, while nouns where the animate plural marker appears as *-iig* (2f) are in class 5 (Nichols 2011). For our purposes, noun classes are the starting point for understanding the basic patterns of nominal inflection in Ojibwe. In the next section, we turn to describing the full range of noun classes to set the stage for a rule-based analysis.

Ojibwe Noun Classes

Noun stems in Ojibwe can be inflected using one of twelve paradigms. Many of these paradigms are similar to one another, save one or two morphemes. However, all inflectional paradigms can be definitively identified by observing the patterns in the following three forms: (1) the singular, which is unmarked (though see discussion below), (2) the plural, which ends in <g> (IPA: /g/) if animate or <n> (IPA: /n/) if inanimate, and (3) the pejorative, which ends in <sh> (IPA: /ʃ/) (Nichols 1980; Valentine 2001; Nichols 2011).[1] These forms are exemplified for each class in example (3).

(3) Class		SG	PL	PEJ
1	a.	esiban 'raccoon'	esibanag	esibanish
	b.	mish-i 'firewood'	mishan	mishish
	c.	giigoonh 'duck'	giigoonhyag	giigoonhyish
2	a.	anishinaabe 'Ojibwe'	anishinaabeg	anishinaabewish
	b.	ikwe 'woman'	ikwewag	ikwewish
3		inini 'man'	ininiwag	ininiwish
4	a.	mitig 'stick'	mitigoog	mitigosh
	b.	amik 'beaver'	amikwag	amikosh
	c.	makw-a 'bear'	makwag	makosh
5		asin 'stone'	asiniig	asiniish
6		mashkimod 'bag'	mashkimodan	mashkimodaash

Class 1 is characterized by consonant-final UNDERLYING stems. At first, this may be surprising when considering the examples in (3), since only Class 1a nouns have singular forms that end in a consonant—Class 1b singular forms end in a short vowel, and Class 1c singular forms end in a long, nasalized vowel. However, in all three cases, Nichols (1980) treats the underlying stem as consonant final. The reasoning is as follows: All Class 1b nouns are disyllabic, and their final vowel is always dropped in suffixed forms; therefore, Nichols assumes that the singular form is derived from a monosyllabic stem, to which a vowel is inserted in the singular to prevent an illegal monosyllabic word. Class 1c nouns are assumed to end in an underlying /y/ (IPA: /j/), which gets predictably deleted in the singular form, but remains in all suffixed forms.

Class 2 is characterized by surface stems that end in a long, non-nasalized vowel. Classes 2a and 2b differ only in plural and obviative forms: Class 2a shows only the final consonant of the suffix, whereas in Class 2b a <w> surfaces before the suffix's initial vowel. Nichols assumes both stems end in an underlying /w/, which must undergo deletion in certain cases since the /w/ does surface in other suffixed forms (1980, 2011). Valentine (2001) does not distinguish 2a and 2b inflectional paradigms; instead, all such stems are treated as long-vowel final, and some Class 2 nouns ending in <e> are grouped into Class 3. This difference in classification is possibly dialectal, since Valentine describes Nishnaabemwin rather than Southwestern Ojibwe.

Class 3 is characterized by a final short vowel in the surface stems. Both Nichols (1980, 2011) and Valentine (2001) assume an underlying /w/ after the short vowel. Other than vowel length, Class 3 stems show the same surface pattern with <w> as Class 2b. For this reason, Nichols only distinguishes Class 3 from Class 2 in later accounts (Nichols 2011).

Class 4 is characterized by a word-final /g/ or /k/ on the surface, which underlying is widely agreed to be followed by a /w/ (Nichols 1980; Valentine 2001; Nichols 2011). Class 4a behaves predictably; Classes 4b and 4c differ only in the plural and obviative, in which the <oo> is replaced by [wa]. Interestingly, stems ending in the same root may not fall in the same class: *amik* 'beaver' and *zaasagokwaanamik* 'fried beaver' are Class 4b, but *waabamik* 'albino beaver' is Class 4a for the same speaker (speaker initials NJ; *Ojibwe People's Dictionary* 2021). Class 4c is similar to 1b in that all singular forms are disyllabic due to the insertion of a final vowel, which does not occur in the suffixed forms.

Class 5 is characterized by suffixed forms that begin with <ii>. Both Nichols (1980, 2011) and Valentine (2001) assume an underlying /y/ (IPA: /j/) at the end of the stem, which gets deleted in singular forms and coalesces with following vowels in the suffixed forms.

Class 6 consists of a small set of irregular consonant-final nouns, which include an 'aa-augment' [-aa-] in all but the diminutive and plural forms (preterit and obviative are unattested in currently available data).

The exact class-labeling convention varies between sources. We follow the most recent labels proposed by Nichols (2011), since they correspond one-to-one with the inflectional patterns exhibited in the language. The relations between conventions are summarized in Table 1.

TABLE 1. Correspondences between labels for the noun inflection classes in Ojibwe

NICHOLS 2011, THIS PAPER	VALENTINE 2001	NICHOLS 1980
Class 1a	Class I	Class 1.1
Class 1b	Class I	Class 1.2a–f
Class 1c	Class I	Class 1.3
Class 2a	Class II	Class 2.3
Class 2b	Class III	Class 2.2
Class 3	Class III	Class 2.1
Class 4a	Class IVa	Class 3.2a–c
Class 4b	Class IVb	Class 3.3a–b
Class 4c	Class IVb	Class 3.1
Class 5	Class V	Class 4
Class 6	Class VI	Class 5.1–5.4

A naive view (one that no modern linguist would seriously defend, and is explicitly rejected by the sources cited above) would be to take noun class labels as not just descriptively useful (which they are), but also PSYCHOLOGICALLY REAL, in the sense that when a speaker of Ojibwe is constructing a plural noun, they first "look up" the class of the noun, then find the allomorph associated with that class. This would mean the lexical storage of not only the class information, but also each distinct allomorph—an inefficiency—and would further make it challenging to understand how novel stems, which would not yet be assigned a class, are readily inflected by proficient speakers in a consistent manner (e.g., as made famous by the Wug Test of Berko 1958). Instead, it is generally agreed that language users store the smallest number of forms possible, and GENERATE allomorphs through the application of general phonological rules.

We turn to an implementation of this approach for Ojibwe noun classes in the next section.

Ingredients and Approach

The approach requires three analytical ingredients: (1) the underlying form of each suffix, (2) the underlying form of each stem, and (3) the phonological rules that apply after suffixes are added. Because phonological rules must apply generally across the language, we keep changes to the phonology from previous accounts to an absolute minimum. Instead, we focus primarily on the possible underlying forms of both the suffixes and the stems. We have only modified phonological rules when no possible combination of underlying forms could make the right empirical predictions.

Suffixal Morphemes

Ojibwe has nine nominal suffix paradigms relevant to this paper, as previously summarized in (1). Each suffix has anywhere from four to six different surface allomorphs, almost exclusively encompassing the 0–2 sonorants at the start of the suffix (Nichols 1980; Valentine 2001; Nichols 2011).

Most affixes go unchanged from previous proposals in our analysis, but there are a few critical divergences that allow for a more general account than has previously been advanced. We treat animate plural and inanimate plural as /-**ag**/ and /-**an**/ respectively, the obviative as /-**an**/, and the locative as /-**ng**/ (following Nichols 1980; Valentine 2001). We assume the diminutive suffix to take a form loosely transcribable as /-**:ns**/, in which the preceding vowel is lengthened and nasalized.

We argue that the person, possessive, preterit, and locative suffixes are all consonant initial rather than i initial (PER /-naan/, /-waa/, /-ni/, POSS /-m/, PRET /-ban/). Nichols (1980) originally argues for this position, but in later work (Nichols 2011) reanalyzes the personal suffixes as /-inaan/, /-iwaa/, and /-ini/, the possessive as /-im/, and the preterit as /-iban/, although the forms are sometimes used interchangeably or with the <i> in parentheses. The two different analyses (with versus without an initial underlying [i]) handle most of the data with about equal power, but there are important differences. If the bolded suffix in (4a) and (5a) is treated as the underlying form, then a rule is needed to DELETE the [i] for (4b) and (5b). If the suffix in (4b) and (5b) is assumed to be the underlying form, then a rule is needed to INSERT the [i] in (4a) and (5a). Which analysis is preferable depends on the underlying form of the stems. For Nichols (2011), the [i]-initial morpheme is necessary to account for the pejorative, but requires the introduction of a class-specific phonological rule. Our account works whether the [i] is part of the suffix or inserted later; however, assuming a consonant-initial suffix is helpful to explain the aa-augment stems (see section titled ACCOUNTING FOR THE NOUN CLASSES).

(4) a. jiimaan 'boat' ni-jiimaan**inaan** 'our boat'
b. -iitaa- 'brother in law' n-iitaa**naan** 'our brother in law'

(5) a. wiyaas 'meat' ni-wiyaas**im** 'my meat'
b. ogimaa 'boss' nind-oogimaa**m** 'my boss'

Finally, we argue that the underlying form of the pejorative suffix is /-ish/. Nichols assumes the initial [i] is epenthesized, although it doesn't make a major difference for his analysis (1980, 2011). Unlike Nichols, it is crucial for our analysis that the [i] is part of the underlying pejorative suffix because it allows us to assume a different underlying form for Class 2a stems (see the next section). This change still predicts the correct allomorphs in other classes while yielding additional explanatory power.

Underlying Stems

Once a suffix is attached, the underlying shape of the stem determines the output allomorph as it defines the context for phonological rules to apply. The shape of the stem does not necessarily correspond to the singular form: Class 1b stems gain an extra vowel in the singular form to prevent monosyllabic words, and Class 1c stems predictably lose their final /y/ when there isn't a suffix to "protect" it (Nichols 1980; Valentine 2001).

Much of our proposal is shared with Nichols (1980). Class 1 stems are assumed to be the default consonant-final stems. Class 1b stems are assumed to be monosyllabic with a vowel inserted to prevent monosyllabic words, and Class 1c is assumed to have a stem-final /y/ that gets deleted in singular forms without a suffix to shield it (see Nichols 1980). Classes 2b, 3, and 4 are still assumed to end with an underlying /w/, and Class 5 stems are still assumed to end in an underlying /y/. These assumptions alone provide predictable environments for phonological rules to apply and allow for the consolidation of several noun classes (see section titled ACCOUNTING FOR THE NOUN CLASSES).

We propose one crucial change to underlying stems: that Class 2a stems end in a long vowel WITHOUT an underlying /w/ (following Bloomfield 1958). Unlike the underlying /w/ in Classes 2b, 3, and 4, the underlying /w/ in Class 2a only appears in two environments: the pejorative and compounds (Nichols 1980), as in (6) and (7):

(6) anishinaabewish
Ojibwe+PEJ
'no-good Ojibwe'

(7) a. ishkotewish
fire+PEJ
'no-good fire' (Nichols 2011)

b. ishkotewapoo
fire+liquid
'whiskey' (Nichols 1980)

Nichols uses this as grounds for an underlying /w/. However, this analysis renders the right boundaries of Class 2a and 2b stems identical, despite their different inflectional paradigms, and necessitates class-specific w-deletion rules (i.e., Rule P-7, see section titled PHONOLOGICAL RULES).

However, assuming Class 2a nouns end in a long vowel correctly predicts all forms except the pejorative and compounds. To generate the correct predictions, we posit a novel w-insertion rule. We turn now to the exposition of these rules.

Phonological Rules

Nichols (1980) describes 35 phonological rules, numbered P-1 to P-35. A list of the rules used in this paper can be found in Appendix 1. Because these rules must apply across the entire language, and our analysis is focused on noun class, we made only minimal changes to prevent proposing rules that have undesirable knock-on effects in other areas of the language.

Our most significant change is the introduction of a novel w-epenthesis rule, which explains the unexpected [w] in Class 2a pejoratives (6–7a) and compounds (7b) mentioned above. We label this P-36 and define it in (8).

(8) **P-36. w-Epenthesis**
The /w/ is inserted after a long vowel occurring before a vowel-initial suffix or compound.

Several strategies for resolving vowel-hiatus are attested in Ojibwe (for discussion, see Newell and Piggot 2014), so the conditions triggering [w]-insertion are not implausible. This rule is intentionally limited in scope, but is crucially not class-specific. It references only general properties, explaining the limited appearance of [w] without requiring the phonology to reference abstract class labels. So long as the rule applies before P-8, it makes the right predictions without interfering with the rest of the nominal morphology.

We make two other changes to existing rules: first, we specify that rule P-19 must occur before P-18. Nichols does not specify that the numbers correspond to rule ordering, but this is necessary for deriving Class 3 inflections. Second, we broaden rule P-30 to apply before ALL short vowels instead of just /ya/. Because we argue the pejorative takes the form /-ish/, this broadening is necessary to predict the correct form. Such a rule would also be necessary to derive the correct forms if any suffixes are presumed to begin with /i/, as in Nichols (2011).

(9) **P-30. Y-contraction (edited)**
Interconsonantal /yV/ and /y/ contract to /ii/.

Summarizing both our proposal for underlying forms and phonological rules, we make the following claims: (1) Class 2a nouns do not have an underlying /w/; instead, the /w/ is inserted to resolve vowel hiatus. (2) Only the pejorative suffix begins with /i/; in all other cases, the [i] is epenthesized. (3) An existing rule that contracts /y/ and /ya/ to [ii) between consonants (P-30) also applies to /yi/. And (4), rule P-19 occurs before rule P-18. These changes alone allow us to derive the majority of Ojibwe's noun suffix allomorphs using phonology alone, with a small class of irregular nouns being the exception.

Accounting for the Noun Classes

Although a noun's inflection cannot be determined by its surface singular form, we argue that eight of the eleven inflectional paradigms can be fully derived phonologically, namely, Classes 1–4a and Class 5. Class 4b–c cannot be derived from basic phonological rules without assuming two different kinds of underlying /w/. Class 6 consists solely of irregular aa-augment nouns; however, our modified phonological rules do provide a predictable phonological environment for aa-augmentation to occur.

The derivation of each class can be summarized in the diagram in Figure 1.

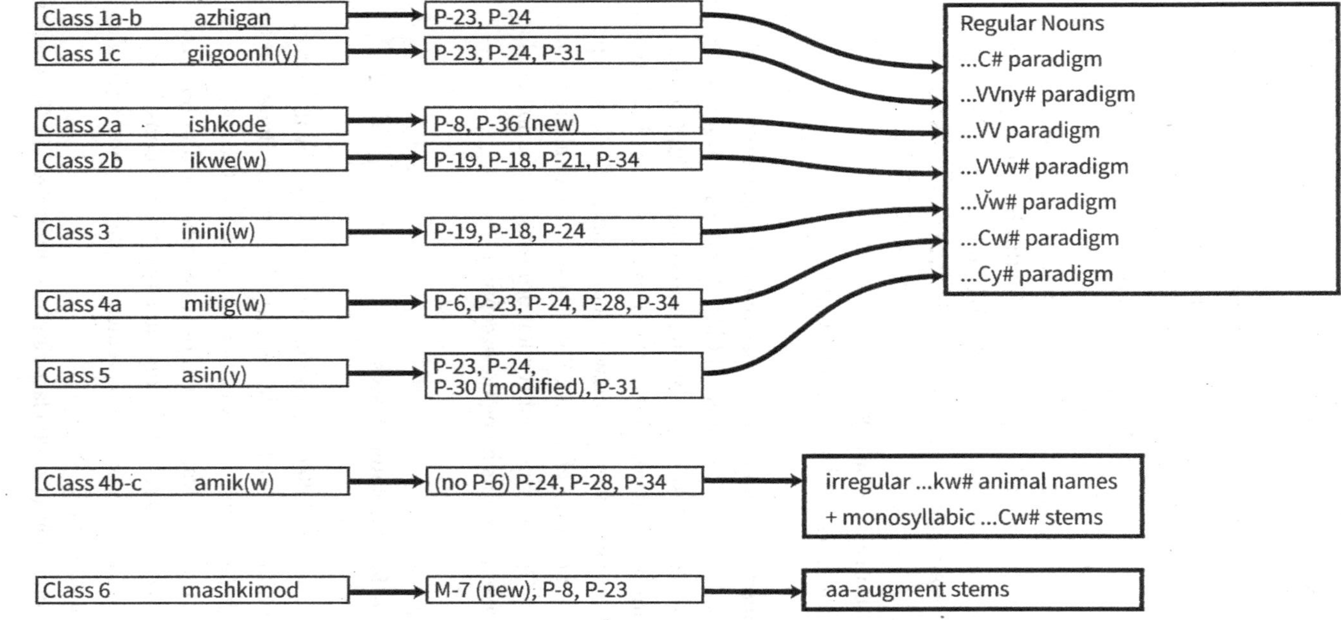

FIGURE 1. A schematization of the underlying forms of each class, and the rules that apply to derive the final surface form.

The arrows point from a class of nouns to the phonological rules that apply to their suffixed forms, then to the resulting paradigm. Most classes reduce into part of the regular paradigm, and the two exceptions remain irregular paradigms. A final note: Except when otherwise indicated, all data in this section comes from the *Ojibwe People's Dictionary* (2021).

Deriving Class 1

All Class 1 stems can be derived phonologically given our assumptions in the section titled INGREDIENTS AND APPROACH. We demonstrate this in example (10) using Class 1a stems. The plural (10c), pejorative (10f), and obviative (10h) are all vowel initial, so they attach with no phonological change. Because no vowel precedes the diminutive (10e), short non-palatalizing [e] is inserted, then lengthened (P-23). Now, only the personal (10a), possessive (10b), locative (10d), and preterit (10g) are consonant initial, so an [i] is inserted (P-24). The same process applies to Class 1b, since the singular suffix is not present in the stem.

(10) a. jiimaan 'boat' — o-jiimaan-**ini** 'his boat'
b. wiyaas 'meat' — ni-wiyaas-**im** 'my meat' (Nichols 2011)
c. azhigan 'sock' — azhigan-**an** 'socks (INAN)'
d. azhigan 'sock' — azhigan-**ing** 'sock+LOC'
e. azhigan 'sock' — azhigan-**ens** 'little sock' (Nichols 2011)
f. azhigan 'sock' — azhigan-**ish** 'no-good sock' (Nichols 2011)
g. -ookomis- 'grandmother' — nookomis-**iban** 'my late grandmother'
h. zhiishiib 'duck' — zhiishiib-**an** 'duck+OBV'

This prediction also applies to Class 1c, with the sole difference being that the /y/ that normally gets deleted in the singular is visible immediately before the suffix. Examples (11b,e,g) show suffixation with no phonological change, example (11d) demonstrates the same sort of e-insertion as (10e), and examples (11a,c,f) show the same sort of i-epenthesis as (10a,b,d,g) (Class 1c person suffixation is not in the currently available data).

(11) a. giigoonh 'fish' ni-giigooy-**im** 'my fish'
b. giigoonh 'fish' giigoonhy-**ag** 'fishes (ANIM)'
c. giigoonh 'fish' giigoonhy-**ing** 'fish+LOC'
d. abinoojiinh 'child' abinoojiiy-**ens** 'little child'
e. giigoonh 'fish' giigoony-**ish** 'no-good fish'
f. mindimooyenh 'old woman' mindimooyeny-i**ban** 'late old woman'
g. giigoonh 'fish' giigoony-**an** 'fish+OBV'

Deriving Class 2

Assuming Class 2a ends in a long vowel WITHOUT an underlying /w/ predicts very few phonological rules need apply. The suffixes in (12a,b,d,e,g) all attach without triggering any general phonological rules. Most notable is the pejorative suffix (12f), which triggers our new w-insertion rule P-36 (see section titled PHONOLOGICAL RULES). However, the plural and obviative suffixes (12c and h, respectively) fall outside the environment specified by P-36, so the initial vowel of each suffix is deleted (P-8).

(12) a. -iitaa- 'brother-in-law' w-iitaa-**ni** 'his brother-in-law'
b. bimide 'grease' ni-bimide-**m** 'my grease' (Nichols 2011)
c. ishkode 'fire' ishkode-**n** 'fires (INAN)'
d. ishkode 'fire' ishkode-**ng** 'fire+LOC'
e. ishkode 'fire' ishkode-**ns** 'little fire'
f. ishkode 'fire' ishkode-**wish** 'no-good fire' (Nichols 2011)
g. anishinaabe 'Ojibwe' anishinaabe-**ban** 'late Ojibwe' (Nichols 2011)
h. anishinaabe 'Ojibwe' anishinaabe-**n** 'Ojibwe+OBV' (Nichols 2011)

This analysis explains why all suffixes except the pejorative treat the stem as vowel final: the stem is vowel final, but a very narrow phonological rule inserts a [w] before the initial vowel of the pejorative suffix can be deleted by P-8.[2] Treating Class 2a as vowel final thus lets us generalize Class 2b as the regular paradigm for VVw-final stems, as demonstrated in (13). Only the vowel-initial plural (13b), pejorative (13e), and obviative (13g) fail to trigger any phonological rules. The rest of the forms are consonant initial and, thus, trigger pre-non-syllabic w-loss, which deletes /w/ between a long vowel and a nonsyllabic consonant (P-21).

(13) a. -oogimaa- 'boss' nind-oogimaa-**m** 'my boss' (Nichols 2011)
b. ikwe 'woman' ikwew-**ag** 'women (ANIM)'
c. ikwe 'woman' ikwe-**ng** 'woman+LOC' (Nichols 2011)
d. ikwe 'woman' ikwe-**ns** 'little woman'
e. ikwe 'woman' ikwew-**ish** 'no-good woman'
f. ikwe 'woman' ikwe-**ban** 'late woman' (Nichols 2011)
g. ikwe 'woman' ikwew-**an** 'woman+OBV' (Nichols 2011)

Deriving Class 3

Class 3 consists entirely of short-vowel-final stems followed by a /w/ that gets deleted in the singular form. All inflections can be derived from our starting assumptions in the section titled INGREDIENTS AND APPROACH, as demonstrated in (14). The vowel-initial suffixes in (14b,e,g) attach with no change. The possessive, locative, and diminutive suffixes in (14a,c,d) begin with consonant clusters or fortis consonants, which lengthen the preceding vowel (P-19). Then, the /w/ is deleted, resulting in the long vowels seen below (P-18). For this derivation to work, P-19 must occur before P-18, otherwise the /w/ deletes before P-19 can apply. These sound rules do not apply to the preterit in (14f) because /b/ is not a fortis consonant. Instead, [i] is inserted (P-24).

(14) a. mashkikii 'pill' mashkikii-**m** 'my pill' (Nichols 2011)
b. inini 'man' ininiw-ag 'men (anim)'
c. inini 'man' ininii-ng 'man+loc' (Nichols 2011)
d. inini 'man' ininii-ns 'little man'
e. inini 'man' ininiw-ish 'no-good man'
f. inini 'man' ininiw-iban 'late man' (Nichols 2011)
g. inini 'man' ininiw-**an** 'man+OBV' (Nichols 2011)

Whether P-19 and P-18 are necessarily two separate rules is unclear. Unless there is other evidence for these rules, it may be more accurate to describe the /w/ as coalescing with the previous vowel rather than lengthening and deleting.

Deriving Class 4

Class 4a can be fully derived using general phonological rules, although every suffixation triggers at least one sound change, as demonstrated in (15). The first rule to apply occurs in the plural and obviative (15c,h): both suffixes begin with /a/, which predictably coalesces with the final /w/ of the stem (P-6). The remaining suffixes do not begin with /a/, so short /e/ is inserted before the diminutive in (15e) (P-23) and short /i/ is inserted before the remaining consonant-initial suffixes in (15a,b,d,g) (P-24). The pejorative (15f) already begins with /i/, so no vowel is inserted. Before the diminutive's lengthening occurs, all clusters of /w/ and short /i/ or /e/ between two consonants coalesce into short [o] (P-28), deriving all the correct surface forms.

(15) a. -shkiinzhig- 'eye(s)' o-shkiinzhigo-**ni** 'his eye(s)'
b. nabagisag 'plank' ni-nabagisago-**m** 'my plank' (Nichols 2011)
c. mitig 'tree' mitigo-**og** 'trees (ANIM)'
d. mitig 'stick' mitigo-**ng** 'stick+LOC'
e. mitig 'stick' mitigoo-**ns** 'little stick'
f. mitig 'tree' mitig-**osh** 'no-good tree'
g. mitig 'tree' niinimo-**ban** 'late tree' (Nichols 2011)
h. mitig 'tree' mitigo-**on** 'tree+OBV' (Nichols 2011)

Class 4b–c, however, cannot be derived using rule-based phonology. All inflections are identical to (15): the only difference is that phonological rule P-6 does not occur, resulting in direct suffixation, as shown in (16a) and obviative (16b).

(16) a. amik 'beaver' amikw-**ag** 'beavers (ANIM)'
b. makwa 'bear' makw-**an** 'bear+OBV'

Rule-based phonology alone cannot account for the differences between Classes 4a and 4b–c without assuming one class has a different kind of /w/ that gets ignored by P-6. This is not impossible; 4a's /w/ could be derived from a former nonmoraic /o/, or the small set of 4b–c nouns could have retained an old inflectional paradigm (as Nichols observes, Class 4b nouns are almost entirely, perplexingly, disyllabic animal names, which suggests a pattern to their inflection). Nonetheless, that the ~30 Class 4b–c nouns ignore a regular phonological rule that otherwise applies generally across the language suggests either an irregular class or incorrect starting assumptions. For simplicity, we assume the former, but leave the question open for discussion.

Deriving Class 5

Class 5 is characterized by an underlying /y/ following a consonant that gets deleted in the singular (P-31). We demonstrate the inflectional forms in (17). The consonant-initial suffixes have a short /e/ (17e) or /i/ (17a,b,g) inserted (P-23, P-24). Then, the underlying /y/ contracts with the following vowel between consonants to form /ii/ (P-30). This results in the predicted forms below.

(17) a. -niji- 'hand(s)' o-niji-**ini** 'his hand(s)'
b. aki 'land' nind-aki-**im** 'my land' (Nichols 2011)
c. asin 'stone' asini-**ig** 'stones (ANIM)'
d. asin 'stone' asini-**ing** 'stone+LOC'
e. asin 'stone' asini-**ins** 'little stone'
f. asin 'stone' asini-**ish** 'no-good stone'
g. -niji- 'hand(s)' ni-ninji-**iban** 'his former hands' (Nichols 2011)
h. asin 'stone' asini-**in** 'stone+OBV'

Note how our modification of rule P-30, as detailed in the section titled PHONOLOGICAL RULES, allows for contraction across the suffixes. Nichols (1980) keeps the scope of this rule narrow and only applies it to /y/ and /ya/. However, broadening the rule to any short vowel allows contraction to occur after i-insertion, and additionally accounts for the pejorative. We assume y-contraction occurs after nasal consonants nasalize their preceding long vowels, then delete (P-29), since y-contraction does not occur in Class 1c nouns.

Deriving Class 6

Class 6 consists solely of the irregular aa-augment nouns, which include [aa] in some inflectional forms. By definition, this class is irregular: its inflectional form is lexically determined. However, our assumptions about the suffixes make aa-insertion more predictable. In (18), [aa] is inserted before the person suffixes (18a), the possessive suffix (18b), the locative suffix (18d), and the pejorative suffix (18f). The forms in (18a–d,g) can be explained if we assume that /aa/ is inserted before a consonant-initial suffix. The forms in (18e–f) do not follow this generalization. One possible explanation is that [aa] was once inserted before consonant-initial suffixes when the diminutive was vowel initial and the pejorative was consonant initial, and the remnants of the system are fossilized in a now-irregular paradigm. Nonetheless, we believe there is no diachronic phonological process that can explain this irregular class; we make no claims about its segmentation.

(18) a. -nik- 'arm' o-nikaa**ni** 'his arm(s)' (Nichols 2011)
b. mashkimod 'bag' ni-mashkimoda**am** 'my bag' (Nichols 2011)
c. mashkimod 'bag' mashkimod**an** 'bags (INAN)'
d. mashkimod 'bag' mashkimoda**ang** 'bag+LOC'
e. mashkimod 'bag' mashkimod**ens** 'little bag'
f. mashkimod 'bag' mashkimoda**ash** 'no-good bag'
g. mashkimod 'bag' mashkimod**an** 'bag+OBV'

Conclusion

In this paper, we distilled the allomorphy in the twelve Ojibwe noun classes (with the exception of two irregular classes) into a predictable system through the examination of three fundamental factors: (1) the underlying form of the suffixal morphemes, (2) the underlying form of the stem, and (3) the general phonological rules of Ojibwe. We assume suffixes take the following forms (those that differ from Nichols (2011) have been bolded): PER /-**naan**/, /-**waa**/, /-**ni**/; POSS /-**m**/; PL.ANIM /-ag/; PL.INAN /-an/; LOC /-ng/; DIM /-*:ns*/; PEJ /-ish/; PRET /-**ban**/; OBV /an/. Most stems are treated in the same manner as in Nichols (1980, 2011) except for Class 2a (e.g., *anishinaabe*, *ishkode*), which we treat as long-vowel final rather than w final (following Bloomfield 1958; Valentine 2001). We only make minor changes to the general phonological rules proposed by Nichols (1980): y-contraction (P-30) causes /y/ and /yV/ to coalesce to /ii/ between consonants (as opposed to /y/ and /ya/), and a new w-epenthesis rule inserts a /w/ between a long vowel and certain vowel-initial suffixes to resolve vowel hiatus.

Overall, the approach captures the phonological similarities between certain stems without the use of descriptive noun classes. More importantly, it allows the phonological rules proposed by Nichols (1980) to largely function without referencing abstract descriptive classes. Nichols (2011) explicitly rejects the notion that these noun classes are psychologically real, and we agree with this position; therefore describing their behavior using general rules is directly beneficial to our understanding of how the phonology and morphology of Ojibwe function.

We highlight that two noun classes cannot be accounted for using rule-based phonology: Class 6 and Class 4b–c (we treat Class 4c as a subset of 4b). Class 6 is definitionally irregular; at least the PER, POSS, LOC, and PEJ suffixes are preceded by a long vowel [aa] (called "aa-augment" by Nichols 1980, 2011). Phonology alone cannot explain the addition of a long [aa], so the class must be lexically specified. Class 4b–c is especially unusual because it behaves regularly in most forms; however, its plural and obviative forms do not undergo /wa/ contraction (P-6), which occurs predictably across the rest of the language in both the nominal and verbal paradigms (Nichols 1980). Why a general phonological rule does not apply to a single class of about 30 nouns is unclear (though see discussion in the subsection titled *Deriving Class 4*).

We would like to close by considering a few directions for future work. First, it is important to consider the knock-on effects that the proposed rule modifications and additions might have. The current work focused only on deriving morphophonological allomorphy in the nominal paradigms, but we intend for the rules to apply across the entire language. Second, we hope that the current work can be used to create pedagogical materials for language learners.

For example, learners could be taught to apply and recognize these regular patterns that cut across nominal classes, rather than memorizing the noun class and class patterns of individual nouns. Third, we are currently in the process of developing a technology known as a finite-state transducer (FST) that can automatically inflect nominal stems, as well as parse inflected forms (for related work in Cree, see Snoek et al. 2014). The goal of this work is to create a full morphological parser for Southwestern Ojibwe, which can be used to build tools for language learners such as automatic noun inflectors, and build parsed corpora for researchers and interested community members to conduct studies that probe the different morphosyntactic patterns in the language (e.g., as has been done by Arppe et al. 2020 for Cree).

Appendix 1: Ordered Phonological Rules and Definitions

All rules are copied directly from Nichols (1980) unless otherwise indicated. Changes and new rules proposed in this paper have been **bolded.** In accordance with the nomenclature in Nichols (1980), we label our new rule **P-36.** Notably, these numbers do not represent rule ordering, but ordering is important to get the right result. Under our analysis, rule P-36 must occur before rule P-8, and rule P-19 must occur before rule P-18.

P-5. Prevowel Vowel Loss. A short vowel is lost before a long vowel.
P-6. WA Contraction. Postconsonantal /w/ and /o/ contract to oo with the /a/ of the peripheral suffixes. This occurs without exception in verbs, but in nouns occurs only after (a) stems ending in /Cw/ where C ≠ k; (b) the noun final /-aakkw/; and (c) stems ending in /V(k)k/ except [**irregular kw-final stems**].
P-36. W-Epenthesis. [w] is inserted after a long vowel occurring before a vowel-initial suffix or compound.
P-8. Postvocalic Vowel Loss. A short vowel is lost after a long vowel.
P-19. W Lengthening. A vowel is lengthened in front of /w/ followed by a nonsyllabic. This does not apply before DUBITATIVE II, before PEJORATIVE in nouns, and, in verbs, before OBVIATIVE. Exceptionally the combination /ssi/ + /w/ + /aC/# in independent negatives gives ssiiC.
P-18. Special W Loss. /w/ is lost before consonant clusters and fortis consonants **if preceded by a vowel** (as per Nichols 2011).
P-21. Pre-non-syllabic W Loss. /w/ is lost after a long vowel before a nonsyllabic (except PEJORATIVE).
P-23. E-Epenthesis. Nonpalatalizing i (/E/) is inserted over a morpheme boundary between a nonsyllabic and a consonant-initial inflectional suffix (and certain derivational suffixes). This applies before /w/ in nouns only before /-waa/ 'I-less'.
P-24. I-Epenthesis. Under the same conditions before derivational and stem forming affixes, /i/ is inserted.
P-28. WI Vocalization. /wi/ and /wE/ are vocalized to /o/ between a nonsyllabic and another nonsyllabic or a word boundary.
P-29. Nasalization. A long vowel is nasalized before /ny/. All vowels are nasalized before /n/ followed by a sibilant. In both cases, the /n/ is omitted.
P-30. Y-Contraction. Interconsonantal ~~/ya/~~ /yV/ and /y/ contract to /ii/.
P-31. Postconsonantal Y Loss. Postconsonantal /y/ is lost.
P-32. Diminutive Lengthening. The vowel in front of the diminutive suffix is lengthened and nasalized. Epenthetic /E/ becomes /e/. Exceptionally the noun final /-kan/ merges with /-nss/ to /-kaanss/.

P-34. Final Postvocalic W Loss. Word-final postvocalic /w/ is lost, but the /w/ of a verb
is not affected.

Appendix 2: Summary Table

All rules are from Nichols 1980 unless otherwise indicated. The process of inserting /aa/ in aa-augment forms has been labeled M-7. C represents any consonant allowed in the position under discussion. V indicates any vowel allowed in the discussed position (VV represents a long vowel, and V represents a short vowel). Grey cells indicate that the predicted forms are unattested (either because no data could be found or because the forms do not exist). **Bold** text indicates a change proposed in this paper (to an affix, class, or rule). Empty cells indicate that the suffix is attached directly without phonological change.

TABLE 2. A summary of the phonological rules that derive each of the noun classes in Ojibwe

	C FINAL	VVNY FINAL	Vv FINAL	VVw FINAL	Vw FINAL	Cw FINAL	Cy FINAL	IRREG. KW	IRREG. C
PER -naan, -waa, -ni	P-23	P-23	-	P-21	P-19, P-18	P-24, P-28	P-30	P-24, P-28	M-7
POSS -m	P-24	P-24	-	P-21	P-19, P-18	P-24, P-28	P-30	P-24, P-28	M-7
PL -ag/-an	-	-	P-8	-	-	P-6	P-30	-	-
LOC -ng	P-24	P-24	-	P-21	P-19, P-18	P-24, P-28	P-30	P-24, P-28	M-7
DIM -:ns	P-23	P-23	-	P-21	P-19, P-18	P-24, P-28	P-30	P-24, P-28	P-23
PEJ -ish	-	-	**P-36**	-	-	P-28	**P-30**	P-28	**M-7, P-8**
PRET -ban	P-24	P-24	-	P-21	P-24	P-24, P-28	P-30	P-24, P-28	M-7
OBV -an	-	-	P-8	-	-	P-6	P-30	-	-

NOTES

1. We follow the following conventions: examples written in the double vowel orthography, which provides an intuitive broad transcription of the actual surface form as spoken, are in italics; brackets [X] are for the surface form, slashes /X/ are for the underlying form, and angle brackets <X> are for orthographic form. IPA is occasionally used as marked.
2. A similar rule has been proposed for the closely related language Plains Cree, where /w/ is inserted after long vowels in borrowed French and English names (Wolvengrey 2011:175). We take this as converging evidence the supports the general plausibility of the proposed analysis.

REFERENCES

Arppe, Antti, Katherine Schmirler, Atticus G. Harrigan, and Arok Wolvengrey. 2020. A Morphosyntactically Tagged Corpus for Plains Cree. *Papers of the Forty-Ninth Algonquian Conference*, ed. by Monica Macaulay and Margaret Noodin, pp. 1–16. East Lansing: Michigan State University Press.

Berko, Jean. 1958. The Child's Learning of English Morphology. *Word* 14(2–3):150–177.

Bloomfield, Leonard. 1958. *Eastern Ojibwa*, ed. by Charles F. Hockett. Ann Arbor: University of Michigan Press.

Newell, Heather, and Glyne Piggot. 2014. Interactions at the Syntax–Phonology Interface: Evidence from Ojibwe. *Lingua* 150:332–362. https://doi.org/10.1016/j.lingua.2014.07.020.

Nichols, John D. 1980. Ojibwe Morphology. PhD thesis, Harvard University.

Nichols, John D. 2011. Concise Grammar of Minnesota Ojibwe. Unpublished manuscript, University of Minnesota-Twin Cities.

Ojibwe People's Dictionary. 2021. Department of American Indian Studies, University of Minnesota. https://ojibwe.lib.umn.edu/.

Snoek, Conor, Dorothy Thunder, Kaidi Lõo, Antti Arppe, Jordan Lachler, Sjur Moshagen, and Trond Trosterud. 2014. Modeling the Noun Morphology of Plains Cree. *Proceedings of the 2014 Workshop on the Use of Computational Methods in the Study of Endangered Languages*, ed. by Jeff Good, Julie Hirschberg, and Owen Rambow, pp. 34–42. Baltimore: Association for Computational Linguistics.

Valentine, J. Randolph. 2001. *Nishnaabemwin Reference Grammar*. Toronto: University of Toronto Press.

Wolvengrey, Arok E. 2011. Semantic and Pragmatic Functions in Plains Cree Syntax. PhD thesis, Universiteit van Amsterdam.

Variation in Prosodic Structure across Algonquian

Natalie Weber, Antti Arppe, Ksenia Bogomolets, Andrew Cowell, Rose-Marie Déchaine, Christopher Hammerly, Sarah E. Murray, Katherine Schmirler, and Rachel Vogel

We report on the motivation, methods, and preliminary findings of a new Algonquian Prosodic Structure Working Group (established spring 2022).[1] This group includes researchers of five Algonquian languages—Arapaho, Blackfoot, Cheyenne, Ojibwe, and Plains Cree—with plans to expand to other languages. Our current focus compares phonological generalizations at morpheme edges in order to determine the prosodic structure of each language. By considering related languages with similar morphosyntax, our eventual aim is to determine how the grammar of prosodic structure may vary and how it is constrained.

Our preliminary results show that each of the five languages exhibits different phonological generalizations at the preverb–stem versus initial–final boundaries, even though the specific phonological processes vary across the languages. For languages where phonological descriptions exist, our findings often confirm those descriptions, but sometimes raise possible alternative morphophonological analyses. For other languages our findings are novel. We argue there are at least two possible prosodic structures within Algonquian: preverbs may be parsed as separate prosodic constituents or as prosodic adjuncts.

In the next section, we motivate our research project and broader goals. After this, we explain our assumptions about prosodic structure and how this structure relates to the Algonquian template. We then detail our methods of investigation and preliminary results before concluding.

Motivating Factors

Why a Within-Family Approach?

The phonology of utterances is widely recognized as having a relationship to morphosyntactic structure, showing isomorphism in some cases and mismatches in others (cf. Kaisse 1985; Nespor and Vogel 2007 [1986]). Early work on prosodic phonology relied on language typology to illuminate points of parametric variation in grammar (Peperkamp 1997; Nespor and Vogel 2007 [1986]; Selkirk 1986, 1996). However, it is difficult to determine whether variation in prosodic structure across different languages derives from differences in syntax or differences in the phonological grammar. Our approach is to study languages within a single language family with similar morphosyntactic templates. This largely eliminates the variable of syntax, and differences in prosodic structure are thus likely derived from different phonological grammars.

Why Algonquian Languages?

Over the last decade there has been a renewed interest in prosodic structure and how it relates to syntactic structure (for example, Match Theory in Selkirk 2011 and overviews of the field in Bennett and Elfner 2019 and Elfner 2018). Recent work has begun to focus on polysynthetic languages, because they exhibit many properties that are useful for testing various theories of syntax–prosody correspondence at the word and phrase levels (e.g., Bogomolets 2020, 2021; Miller 2018; Miller and Sande 2021; Weber 2020, 2022; and case studies in Bogomolets and van der Hulst 2023). Relative to Algonquian languages, words contain extreme phonological length and morphosyntactic complexity, extensive agglutinative morphology, free word order, multiple "lexical" morphemes or roots within a morphological word, and head-marking (see Baker 1996; Mattissen 2004; Nichols 1986), as well as "word"-internal syntactic adjuncts (Déchaine and Weber 2018; Fenger 2020; Mathieu et al. 2017; Piggott and Travis 2013; Weber 2022).

Why Now?

A comparative project of this size was not possible until now, because many Algonquian languages only recently received rich documentation, especially thanks to computational tools. This documentation includes lexical resources and speech corpora we can use to probe for prosodic structure. Lexical resources are excellent for determining segmental alternations across paradigms but often include no information about suprasegmentals, such as stress, pitch, and intonation. Speech corpora may not include systematic data that could be used to build paradigms, but contain rich information on suprasegmental properties.

Relating Prosodic and Morphosyntactic Structure

In this section we discuss our assumptions about prosodic structure, the basic morphosyntactic structure of Algonquian languages, and our hypotheses about how the two correspond.

Prosodic Structure

Linguistic utterances consist of hierarchical sets of units. These units organize into hierarchical prosodic structures that derive from—but are not necessarily isomorphic with—syntax (Downing 1999; Hall 1999; Hayes 1989; Inkelas 1990; Itô and Mester 2012; Kaisse 1985; Kiparsky 1982; Nespor and Vogel 2007 [1986]; Pierrehumbert and Beckman 1988; Selkirk 1984, 1986, 2011). We analyze the prosodic structure of the Algonquian verbal complex in terms of two "word"-level prosodic categories of the Prosodic Hierarchy: Prosodic Word (PWd) and Prosodic Stem (PStem).

These prosodic units define the domains for phonological processes and generalizations, including segmental alternations and prosodic information like stress and phrasal pitch contours. In our current work, we focus on segmental alternations at morpheme edges, and use these to infer the presence of prosodic boundaries and constituents, as detailed in the Methods section. The prosodic constituents correspond to spans of positions on the complex Algonquian verbal template, to which we turn next.

The Algonquian Template

A simplified template for verbal complexes is given in (1) and exemplified with Plains Cree words (Wolvengrey 2001; see Bloomfield 1946 and Goddard 1990 for the Algonquian template). The stem (in brackets) is prototypically multimorphemic, with morphemes named by their position within the stem (e.g., "initial" and "final"). The initial is minimally and prototypically a root, while the final is a verbalizing *v* head (e.g., Branigan et al. 2005; Brittain 2003; Bruening 2001:122; Hirose 2003; Mathieu 2007; Quinn 2006; Slavin 2012). "Preverbs" are a heterogeneous class of grammatical and lexical morphemes. The stem and preverbs may be preceded and followed by inflectional affixes marking person and other grammatical categories. This template abstracts away from more complex details; each position may itself be morphologically complex, and there may be other positions not shown here, such as prefinals, postradicals, and so on.

(1) Plains Cree (Arppe et al. 2022; Wolvengrey 2001)

person-	preverbs-	[initial	-final]$_{\text{stem}}$	-suffixes	
		pim	-ohtê	-w	'S/he walks along.'
	sâpo-	pim	-ohtê	-w	'S/he walks past.'
ki-	sâpo-	pim	-ohtâ	-n	'You walk past.'

An open question is how these position classes map onto different prosodic constituents, to which we turn next.

Relation between Prosodic Structure and the Template

Previous work on Algonquian prosodic structure has focused on mapping syntactic analyses to prosodic structure, with less focus on whether phonological processes correlate to that structure (Branigan et al. 2005; Mathieu et al. 2017; Piggott and Travis 2013; Russell 1999; Russell and Reinholtz 1997). In contrast, we focus on deriving prosodic structure in a "bottom up" fashion based on phonological generalizations that hold across positions in the morphosyntactic template. A key question is whether such templates constitute a single undifferentiated structure (H1), or whether they contain a single core structure with adjuncts attached (H2), or whether they contain multiple units (H3). These three hypotheses are shown in (2), although they do not exhaust all possible hypotheses about how the morphological template could be parsed into prosodic structure.

(2) Hypotheses about prosodic structure relative to the Algonquian template

H1 ((prefixes- preverb- initial -final -suffixes)$_{PStem}$)$_{PWd}$

H2 (prefixes- preverb- (initial -final -suffixes)$_{PStem}$)$_{PWd}$

H3 (prefixes- (preverb-)$_{PStem}$ (initial -final -suffixes)$_{PStem}$)$_{PWd}$

To probe for prosodic structure, we consider domain-delimited phonological generalizations across the templatic positions. We assume that if two domains—that is, two strings of templatic positions—exhibit the same phonological generalizations, then both domains are parsed into prosodic structure in the same way. In this way we determine a set of prosodic structures for each language which are compatible with the generalizations. The resulting structures can then be compared across languages.

Methods

This section outlines our process of annotating textual resources in order to determine phonological generalizations at morpheme boundaries. We describe in detail how we map those generalizations to a prosodic structure, using an illustration from Cheyenne.

Resources

Our resources include textual and audio data structures. The textual data come primarily from dictionaries, grammars, and annotated corpora (Blackfoot: Frantz and Russell 2017; Genee and Junker 2018; Weber et al. 2023; Cheyenne: Fisher et al. 2006; Arapaho: Cowell and Moss 2008; Salzmann et al. 2012; Plains Cree: Wolvengrey 2001; https://itwewina.altlab.app [Arppe et al. 2022]; https://korp.altlab.app [Arppe et al. 2020]; Ojibwe: Ojibwe People's Dictionary 2022).

We extracted fully inflected words into spreadsheets and added a surface morphemic analysis. We then annotated each word with unique underlying forms (URs) for each morpheme. These URs were frequently created by us during the annotation process, although some lexical resources already included morphemic analyses which we could use or modify. The URs allowed us to sort inflected words into derivational paradigms of preverbs, initials, and finals "on the fly." In this way we were able to easily see morphophonological alternations, from which we posit phonological generalizations regarding different templatic positions. An excerpt of the spreadsheet for Ojibwe is shown in Table 1, sorted by the "Final UR" column to sort words with the final *-abi* 's/he sits, stays' together.[2] The fifth column is a surface analysis of the orthographic word into morphemes. The examples in this column show that the final is *-abi* after consonants, but *-bi* after long vowels. (Ojibwe <e> and doubled letters are long vowels.) Spreadsheets like this allow us to see that there is an alternation *-abi* ~ *-bi*, to posit an underlying form /-abi/ 'sit, stay' and a deletion rule that we return to in our results section. For Ojibwe, this frequently confirms the UR in the Ojibwe People's Dictionary (2022), but for some of the other languages these analyses are novel.

One potential confound is that the textual resources are written in various vernacular orthographies, which tend to be conservative and obscure details of pronunciation such as speaker variation or surface-level allophony. Orthographic conventions also tend to be based on implicit knowledge of the Algonquian position classes (e.g., in some orthographies a hyphen is used to demarcate preverbs, which suggests particular phonological generalizations that may not be accurate or well described). To address this, in the future we plan to create phonetic transcriptions for analysis whenever the lexical resources include systematic audio files. Systematic

TABLE 1. Partial annotated spreadsheet for Ojibwe

INITIAL UR	INITIAL GLOSS	FINAL UR	FINAL GLOSS	SURFACE ANALYSIS	GLOSS
aasw-	leaning against	-abi	s/he sits, stays	aasw-abi	s/he sits leaning against something
ap-	onto or against something	-abi	s/he sits, stays	ap-abi	s/he sits on something
deb-	enough, adequate, reach	-abi	s/he sits, stays	deb-abi	s/he has enough room to sit
apiit-	to a certain extent, degree, rate, or speed	-abi	s/he sits, stays	apiit-abi	s/he comes up to a certain height when seated
zhig-	urinate	-abi	s/he sits, stays	zhig-abi	s/he urinates sitting
anwe-	rest	-abi	s/he sits, stays	anwe-bi	s/he rests
ishkwe-	at the end, last	-abi	s/he sits, stays	ishkwe-bi	s/he sits at the end
giizhoo-	warm	-abi	s/he sits, stays	giizhoo-bi	s/he sits in a warm place, lives in a warm house

paradigms for some alternations may only be available by working with speakers to record and transcribe forms. However, at the present time we have only worked with written resources, and the process described in the following section reflects these kinds of data sources.

Process

We orient all data generalizations to the traditional Algonquian morphological template and position classes (Bloomfield 1946; Goddard 1990). We define prosodic constituents on the template using standard methods (Hall 1999; Nespor and Vogel 2007 [1986]) by determining phonological generalizations across spans or edges of positions (cf. Tallman 2021). At this stage of our project we restrict ourselves to morphemes in the 'preverb' and 'initial' positions. The reason is that this allows us to diagnose the presence of prosodic boundaries between the preverb and the stem, which is what distinguishes the three hypotheses in (2). Preverbs are frequently described as separate phonological domains within the Algonquian word (Bloomfield 1946:103; Goddard 1990:478), meaning that this boundary is likely to show unique phonological characteristics relative to the initial position in most languages. However, the phonological generalizations that underlie these claims are often left inexplicit or not laid out systematically, which is a gap our research intends to fill.

Many roots freely occur in preverb and initial positions, allowing us to compare morphophonological alternations and the generalizations that drive these alternations in both positions. As a concrete example, consider the root *ame-* 'along' in Cheyenne, in (3), which can occur as an initial or a preverb.[3] (Examples are given in Cheyenne orthography, which is broadly phonemic. Note that <e> is typically pronounced as a high front vowel, though occasionally as a mid front vowel. The overdot represents voicelessness.)

(3) Cheyenne (Fisher et al. 2006)

prefix-	preverbs-	[initial	-final]$_{stem}$	-suffixes	Translation
É-		[**ame**	-méohe]		'He's running.'
É-		[sóhp	-a'xe]		'He took off.'
É-	**amė-**	[sóhp	-a'xe]		'He ran by.'

In the initial position, (4), the root is *ame-* before consonants and *am-* before vowels. In the preverb position, (5), the root is *ame-* regardless of the following segments.

(4) Cheyenne root *am-* ~ *ame-* 'along' in initial position
É-[**ame**-tó'hóna]. 'He's swimming by.'
É-[**am**-évone]. 'The sound went by.'

(5) Cheyenne root *ame-* 'along' in preverb position
É-**ame**-[táhoo'e]. 'He's riding along.'
É-**ame**-[é'kotsen]-óho. 'He's got his arm around her as he walks along.'

In the initial position, there is an <e> ~ Ø alternation at the right edge of this root, which avoids consonant or vowel sequences across the initial–final morpheme boundary. In the preverb position, this root ends invariably in <e>. To our knowledge, these morphophonological alternations have not been laid out systematically, as in (4) and (5), nor described phonologically in this way for Cheyenne.

We conclude from this that there is a prosodic boundary at the right edge of preverbs with a phonotactic restriction against <m>. This explains why *ame-* 'along' never alternates with *am-* in this position. There is also some prosodic domain that includes the initial and final positions (and possibly more) where consonant and vowel sequences are avoided across morpheme boundaries. This partial prosodic structure is shown in (6), with the known prosodic boundaries shown with parentheses. Because this structure is based on a single root alternation, we abstract away from the question of what to label the prosodic domains in (6). Even so, the right edge boundary after the preverb means that this partial prosodic structure is only compatible with H3 from (2), or something like it.

(6) Partial prosodic structure in Cheyenne
prefixes- preverb-) (initial -final -suffixes

By considering a number of different roots that exhibit different processes, we are able to create more accurate phonological generalizations and to build up a fuller picture of the prosodic structure.

Results

In this section we present preliminary findings using the methods described above, with a focus on phonological generalizations at the edges of the preverb and initial positions. We show that despite their similar morphosyntax, these languages exhibit variation in terms of phonological evidence and prosodic structure.

Generalizations about Initials

All five languages exhibit a set of alternations at the right edge of initials. These are not yet fully enumerated, but frequently involve consonant and vowel alternations with zero, some of which were described in earlier work (e.g., Bloomfield 1946:90–93). Most languages are said to have some form of vowel epenthesis between consonants, though we have found that the alternations in some languages are compatible with alternative analyses. We focus here on Ojibwe, since the environments for epenthesis and palatalization are well described (Kaye and Piggott 1973; Truitner and Dunnigan 1975).

As shown in (7), some finals begin in a short vowel after an initial that ends in a consonant, such as *deb-* 'enough', but that vowel deletes after an initial ending in a long vowel, such as *giizhoo-* 'warm'.[4] Interestingly, some finals with an <i> ~ Ø alternation are analyzed in the Ojibwe People's Dictionary (2022) as beginning in a short vowel, such as *-izi* '(anim.) be', while others begin in a consonant, such as *-shin* 'lie', and the <i> is epenthesized between consonants. On its own, the <i> ~ Ø alternation in (7) cannot explain why *-izi* '(anim.) be' is analyzed as beginning in a vowel and *-shin* is analyzed as beginning in a consonant.

(7) Ojibwe finals beginning in short vowels (Ojibwe People's Dictionary 2022)

/-abi/	deb-abi	'S/he has enough room to sit.'
	giizhoo-bi	'S/he sits in a warm place.'
/-izi/	deb-izi	'S/he is satisfied.'
	giizhoo-zi	'S/he is warm [person].'
/-shin/	deb-ishin	'S/he, it (anim.) lies fitting in.'
	giizhoo-shin	'S/he lies in warmth.'

There is another correlate of epenthesis, which is palatalization of a preceding <t>. In (8), the initial *apiit-* 'so much' occurs with <t> before underlying vowels, but with a <ch> before the epenthetic <i>. Our point here is that the palatalization data is also compatible with the opposite analysis, where palatalization occurs before underlying /i/ but not epenthetic [i]. In fact, this alternative analysis would unite the behavior of underlying short /i/ and long /iˑ/, because palatalization also occurs before long /iˑ/, as in *apiich-ii* 's/he does something at a certain rate or speed'. We believe that a systematic consideration of morpheme alternations such as these may bring other traditional analyses into question.

(8) Ojibwe finals and palatalization (Ojibwe People's Dictionary 2022)

/-abi/	apiit-abi	'S/he comes up to a certain height when seated.'
/-izi/	apiit-izi	'S/he is a certain age.'
/-shin/	apii**ch**-ishin	'S/he, it (anim.) lies so thick.'

Some languages also exhibit alternations at the left edge of initials. Blackfoot initials undergo alternations at the left edge when they occur after a prefix, regardless of whether it ends in a consonant or a vowel. Restricting the discussion to initials that begin in a consonant followed by a short vowel: There is [i]-epenthesis before initials that begin in an obstruent, (9), and there is nasal deletion for initials that begin in nasals, (10).[5]

(9) Blackfoot initials beginning in obstruents (Frantz and Russell 2017:91)

	prefix-	preverbs-	[initial	-final]$_{stem}$	-suffixes	Translation	
a.			**pon**	-ihtáá	-t	'Pay!'	Left edge
b.		áaks-	**ipon**	-ihtaa	-wa	'She will pay.'	After C
		áká-	**ípon**	-ihtsi	-wa	'He is dead.'	After V

(10) Blackfoot initials beginning in nasals (Frantz and Russell 2017:182–183)

	prefix-	preverbs-	[initial	-final]$_{stem}$	-suffixes	Translation	
a.			**mokáki**		-t!	'Be smart!'	Left edge
b.		áak-	**okaki**		-wa	'She will be smart.'	After C
	n-	iká-	**ókaki**	-ssko	-a-wa	'I have "wised him up".'	After V

The alternations in (9) and (10) are summarized in (11). Crucially, there is a separate set of roots that begin in a vowel in all environments, and there are no roots that begin in an obstruent or nasal in all environments, suggesting the roots in (11) begin in an underlying consonant. Thus, there is a conspiracy of processes that avoids [+cons] segments at the juncture between a prefix/preverb and an initial.

(11) Blackfoot root alternations in initial position

UR	Left edge	After C	=	After V	Gloss
/pon-/	pon-	ipon-		ipon-	'cease'
/mokaki-/	mokaki-	okaki-		okaki-	'bring'
(none)	*p, *m	*p, *m		*p, *m	

Generalizations about Preverbs

Four of the five languages (Cheyenne, Arapaho, Plains Cree, Ojibwe, but not Blackfoot) have restrictions at the right edge of preverbs. Cheyenne allows preverbs to end in a vowel, (12a), or a glottal fricative <h> or stop <'>, (12b). Arapaho limits endings to a vowel or a glottal fricative <h>, but not the glottal stop <'>, and Plains Cree and Ojibwe require preverbs to end in a vowel.

(12) a. Cheyenne preverbs ending in vowels

éva-	'back, return'	he'aná-	'easy'
ame-	'along'	he'né-	'spread out, distributed'
hó'ko-	'must'	ȧsó-	'suddenly, in a group'

b. Cheyenne preverbs ending in glottal consonants

mėh-	'could have, would have'
tšėške'-	'little'

This right edge restriction is enforced with active phonological processes, primarily a process that looks like phonological epenthesis. For any initial that alternates between having a right-edge consonant before vowels and a right-edge high vowel before consonants, the related preverb always ends in a final high vowel, as in (13). (For some languages, this generalization holds only at an abstract level, and later processes like coalescence or deletion obscure the preverb-final high front vowel.) Initials that end in a vowel exhibit other patterns of alternation. This suggests that roots like those in (13) end in an underlying consonant, and that a high front vowel is epenthesized at the right edge of preverbs.

(13)

	Initial	Preverb	Gloss
Cheyenne	am- ~ ame-	ame-	'along'
Arapaho	ceb-/cow-[6] ~ cebi-	cebi-	'along'
Plains Cree	pim- ~ pimi-	pimi-	'along'
Ojibwe	bim- ~ bimi-	bimi-	'along'
(none)	*... C- ~ ... Ci-	*... C-	

Our analysis of preverb-final [i] as an epenthetic vowel contrasts with the traditional Bloomfieldian analysis, which treats this vowel as a particle-forming suffix /-i/ that attaches to roots (Bloomfield 1946:103–104,116–117). What our account adds is the observation that the distribution of preverb-final [i] is phonological. First, it occurs after preverbs ending in a consonant (or certain non-glottal consonants in Cheyenne and Arapaho), but not preverbs ending in a vowel. Second, [i] is motivated by a phonological edge restriction: All preverbs must end in a vowel (or certain glottal consonants in Cheyenne and Arapaho). Regardless of whether the [i] is epenthetic or underlying, our argument is that the distribution of [i] provides evidence for a prosodic boundary at the right edge of preverbs in Plains Cree, Ojibwe, Cheyenne, and Arapaho.

In contrast, Blackfoot has no restrictions at the right edge of preverbs, which can end in a vowel (14a), consonant (14b), consonant cluster (14c), or geminate consonant (14d). In addition, the right edge of roots have the same realization in initial and preverb positions in Blackfoot, without alternations.

(14) Blackfoot preverbs ending in . . .

a. Short vowels

sa-	'out'
isimi-	'secretly'
ka'to-	'assist'

b. Consonants

ikkam-	'fast'
paahtsik-	'barely'
miistap-	'away'

c. Consonant clusters

ipo't-	'reciprocal'
pisst-	'inside'
ikkahs-	'humorous, funny'
sska'-	'extremely'

d. Geminate consonants

iss-	'young, in front'
kipp-	'might' (please)
matt-	'again'

Within-Family Variation

Comparison across the five languages reveals parametric variation in prosodic structure. Our findings show that Ojibwe and Plains Cree both have phonotactic restrictions at the right edge of preverbs. This is compatible only with H3 from (2), because only this hypothesis has a prosodic boundary at the right edge of preverbs. Under H3, each preverb is parsed as a separate prosodic domain, converging with previous research (Branigan et al. 2005; Piggott and Travis 2013; Russell 1999). The prosodic structure of Cheyenne and Arapaho is less certain at this time, though not *in*compatible with H3. Blackfoot has no restrictions at the right edge of preverbs, meaning there is no evidence for a prosodic boundary there. Blackfoot is compatible with H2, where the preverb is not parsed into a separate prosodic constituent. This kind of structure explains Blackfoot because we can say that there is a prohibition against [+cons] segments to the right of each juncture outside of the stem+suffixes domain, which forms a separate PStem and which exhibits distinct phonological processes, such as vowel epenthesis only between consonants (Weber 2020:234–259).

These two prosodic structures make different predictions regarding minimal size constraints. A prosodic constituent like the PStem may exhibit a lower bound on size (Downing 1999; Hall 1999; McCarthy and Prince 1999). Lexical preverbs that are Pstems in languages like Plains Cree and Ojibwe are minimally bimoraic. Together with the constraint against consonants at the right edge of preverbs, this means that preverbs are minimally either CVV or CVCV, (15). Blackfoot preverbs are expected to have no minimal size, because Blackfoot preverbs are not parsed to a PStem constituent. Consequently, preverbs in Blackfoot may be as small as V, CV, or VC, (16); see also Weber (2022).

(15) Minimal preverbs in Plains Cree

*V		
*CV		
*VC		
CVV	pê-	'hither'
CVCV	pimi-	'along'

(16) Minimal preverbs in Blackfoot

V	a-	'IPFV'
CV	sa-	'out'
VC	on-	'hurry'

The observations of right edge restrictions and minimal size constraints provide converging evidence that Blackfoot prosodic structure is something like H2 rather than H3 and that there is variation in prosodic structure across Algonquian.

Conclusion

Our findings confirm that all languages in our present study exhibit different phonological generalizations at the preverb–stem versus initial–final boundaries. These differences encompass a range of phonological processes, including epenthesis, deletion, vowel coalescence, and more. We have reported on some of these processes, and continue our work to enumerate others. The processes may target the right edges of preverbs or initials, the left edges, or both edges within a single language.

Our findings also highlight variation in prosodic structure across the five languages. Preverbs are parsed as PStems in Plains Cree and Ojibwe (and probably Cheyenne and Arapaho), but not in Blackfoot. Under our analysis, the difference in prosodic structure results from different phonological grammars, rather than a difference in morphosyntax. We interpret the [i] that follows a preverb in all languages except for Blackfoot as phonologically motivated. This [i] could be analyzed as an epenthetic vowel at the right edge of a PStem equally well as a derivational morpheme /-i/ (e.g., Piggott and Travis 2013). Part of our contribution to Algonquian linguistics is to point out areas where alternative phonological analyses are available.

Finally, our research raises questions about the labels used in our prosodic structures. We have implicitly assumed that the morphological stem maps to a PStem constituent (Downing 1999), with the suffixes typically incorporated into this constituent. These PStems also have many properties typically associated with the PWd, such as minimal size restrictions and generalizations about stress and/or syllabification. Because of this, many researchers label this stem+suffixes domain a PWd (e.g., Russell 1999 for Plains Cree). Our preliminary findings do not answer the question about labels but do show that "word"-like phonological properties in polysynthetic languages are distributed across several prosodic constituents.

NOTES

1. The authors thank the audiences at the 54th Algonquian Conference and the 2023 LSA Annual Meeting for their comments.
2. The full spreadsheet includes columns for each templatic position within words, including the initial and final (shown here), multiple preverbs, and more.
3. We focus here on lexical preverbs and set grammatical preverbs aside for future research

because they tend to exhibit a distinct set of characteristics. Frequently they occur in a fixed order at the left edge of the preverb domain and are phonologically smaller than lexical preverbs.

4. Ojibwe has a short <o> vowel as well, but we could not find clear examples of a final beginning in <o> after a consonant and a long vowel.
5. There are more patterns of alternation for roots that have a long vowel in the first syllable (Weber 2020:261–262).
6. This Arapaho root (underlyingly /cew-/) also has vowel and consonant alternations related to a process of regressive vowel harmony (Cowell and Moss 2008:20–22). This does not affect our argument regarding epenthesis.

REFERENCES

Arppe, Antti, Katherine Schmirler, Atticus G. Harrigan, and Arok Wolvengrey. 2020. A Morphosyntactically Tagged Corpus for Plains Cree. *Papers of the 49th Algonquian Conference*, ed. by Monica Macauley and Margaret Noodin, pp. 1–16. East Lansing: Michigan State University Press.

Arppe, Antti, Jolene Poulin, Eddie Antonio Santos, Andrew Neitsch, Atticus Harrigan, Katherine Schmirler, Daniel Hieber, Ansh Dubey, and Arok Wolvengrey. 2022. *itwêwina*—Towards a Morphologically Intelligent and User-Friendly On-line Dictionary of Plains Cree—Next Next Round. Paper read at the 54th Algonquian Conference, Boulder, CO, 22 October. Available at https://altlab.ualberta.ca/wp-content/uploads/2023/03/itwewina_AC54_Oct2022.pptx.pdf.

Baker, Mark C. 1996. *The Polysynthesis Parameter*. Oxford: Oxford University Press.

Bennett, Ryan, and Emily Elfner. 2019. The Syntax–Prosody Interface. *Annual Review of Linguistics* 5:151–171.

Bloomfield, Leonard. 1946. Algonquian. *Linguistic Structures of Native America*, ed. by Cornelius Osgood. Publications in Anthropology, vol. 6, pp. 85–129. New York: Viking Fund.

Bogomolets, Ksenia. 2020. Lexical Accent in Languages with Complex Morphology. PhD thesis, University of Connecticut.

Bogomolets, Ksenia. 2021. Morphology–Phonology Interplay in Lexical Stress Assignment: Ichishkiin Sɨnwit. *Acta Linguistica Academica* 68(1–2): 77–102.

Bogomolets, Ksenia, and Harry van der Hulst (eds.). 2023. *Word Prominence in Languages with Complex Morphologies*. Oxford: Oxford University Press.

Branigan, Phil, Julie Brittain, and Carrie Dyck. 2005. Balancing Syntax and Prosody in the

Algonquian Verb Complex. *Papers of the 36th Algonquian Conference*, ed. by H. Christoph Wolfart, pp. 75–93. Winnipeg: University of Manitoba.

Brittain, Julie. 2003. A Distributed Morphology Account of the Syntax of the Algonquian Verb. *Proceedings of the 2003 Annual Conference of the Canadian Linguistic Association*, ed. by Stanca Somesfalean and Sophie Burrelle, pp. 25–39. Université du Québec à Montréal.

Bruening, Benjamin. 2001. Syntax at the Edge: Cross-Clausal Phenomena and the Syntax of Passamaquoddy. PhD thesis, Massachusetts Institute of Technology.

Cowell, Andrew, and Alonzo Moss, Sr. 2008. *The Arapaho language*. Boulder: University Press of Colorado.

Déchaine, Rose-Marie, and Natalie Weber. 2018. Root Syntax: Evidence from Algonquian. *Papers of the 47th Algonquian Conference*, ed. by Monica Macaulay and Margaret Noodin, pp. 57–82. East Lansing: Michigan State University Press.

Downing, Laura J. 1999. Prosodic Stem =/= Prosodic Word in Bantu. *Studies on the Phonological Word*, ed. by T. Alan Hall and Ursula Kleinhenz, pp. 73–98. Amsterdam: John Benjamins.

Elfner, Emily. 2018. The Syntax–Prosody Interface: Current Theoretical Approaches and Outstanding Questions. *Linguistics Vanguard* 4(1):20160081. https://doi.org/10.1515/lingvan-2016-0081.

Fenger, Paula. 2020. Words within Words: The Internal Syntax of Verbs. PhD thesis, University of Connecticut.

Fisher, Louise, Wayne Leman, Leroy Pine, Sr., and Marie Sanchez. 2006. *Cheyenne Dictionary*. Lame Deer, MT: Chief Dull Knife College. Updated regularly online at http://www.cdkc.edu/cheyennedictionary/index.html.

Frantz, Donald G., and Norma Jean Russell. 2017. *Blackfoot Dictionary of Stems, Roots, and Affixes*. 3rd ed. Toronto: University of Toronto Press.

Genee, Inge, and Marie-Odile Junker. 2018. The Blackfoot Language Resources and Digital Dictionary Project: Creating Integrated Web Resources for Language Documentation and Revitalization. *Language Documentation & Conservation* 12:274–314.

Goddard, Ives. 1990. Primary and Secondary Stem Derivation in Algonquian. *International Journal of American Linguistics* 56(4):449–483.

Hall, T. Alan. 1999. The Phonological Word: A Review. *Studies on the Phonological Word*, ed. by T. Alan Hall and Ursula Kleinhenz, pp. 1–22. Amsterdam: John Benjamins.

Hayes, Bruce. 1989. The Prosodic Hierarchy in Meter. *Rhythm and Meter*, ed. by Paul Kiparsky and Gilbert Youmans, pp. 201–260. Orlando, FL: Academic Press.

Hirose, Tomio. 2003. *Origins of Predicates: Evidence from Plains Cree*. New York: Routledge.

Inkelas, Sharon. 1990. *Prosodic Constituency in the Lexicon*. New York: Garland.

Itô, Junko, and Armin Mester. 2012. Recursive Prosodic Phrasing in Japanese. *Prosody Matters:*

Essays in Honor of Elisabeth Selkirk, ed. by Toni Borowsky, Shigeto Kawahara, Mariko Sugahara, and Takahito Shinya, pp. 280–303. Sheffield, UK: Equinox Press.

Kaisse, Ellen M. 1985. *Connected Speech: The Interaction of Syntax and Phonology*. New York: Academic Press.

Kaye, Jonathan D., and Glyne L. Piggott. 1973. On the Cyclical Nature of Ojibwa T-Palatalization. *Linguistic Inquiry* 4(3):345–362.

Kiparsky, Paul 1982. From Cyclic Phonology to Lexical Phonology. *The Structure of Phonological Representations*, vol. 1, ed. by Harry van der Hulst and Norval Smith, pp. 131–175. Dordrecht: Foris.

Mathieu, Éric. 2007. Petite syntaxe des finales concrètes en ojibwe. *Papers of the 38th Algonquian Conference*, ed. by H. C. Wolfart, pp. 1–27. Winnipeg: University of Manitoba Press.

Mathieu, Éric, Brandon J. Fry, and Michael Barrie. 2017. Adjunction of Complex Heads inside Words: A Peply to Piggott and Travis (2013). *The Structure of Words at the Interfaces*, ed. by Heather Newell, Máire Noonan, Glyne Piggott, and Lisa deMena Travis, pp. 240–260. Oxford: Oxford University Press.

Mattissen, Johanna. 2004. A Structural Typology of Polysynthesis. *Word* 55(2):189–216.

McCarthy, John J., and Alan Prince. 1999. Faithfulness and Identity in Prosodic Morphology. *The Prosodic Morphology Interface*, ed. by René Kager, Harry van der Hulst, and Wim Zonneveld, pp. 258–267. Cambridge: Cambridge University Press.

Miller, Taylor L. 2018. The Phonology–Syntax Interface and Polysynthesis: A Study of Kiowa and Saulteaux Ojibwe. PhD thesis, University of Delaware.

Miller, Taylor L., and Hannah Sande. 2021. Is Word-Level Recursion Actually Recursion? *Languages* 6(2):100. https://doi.org/10.3390/languages6020100.

Nespor, Marina, and Irene Vogel. 2007 [1986]. *Prosodic Phonology*. 2nd edn. New York: Mouton de Gruyter.

Nichols, Johanna. 1986. Head-Marking and Dependent-Marking Grammar. *Language* 62(1):56–119.

Ojibwe People's Dictionary. 2022. https://ojibwe.lib.umn.edu.

Peperkamp, Sharon Andrea. 1997. *Prosodic Words*. The Hague: Holland Academic Graphics.

Pierrehumbert, Janet, and Mary Beckman. 1988. *Japanese Tone Structure*. Cambridge, MA: MIT Press.

Piggott, Glyne, and Lisa Travis. 2013. Adjuncts within Words and Complex Heads. *Syntax and its Limits*, ed. by Raffaella Folli, Christina Sevdali, and Robert Truswell, pp. 157–174. Oxford: Oxford University Press.

Quinn, Conor. 2006. Referential-Access Dependency in Penobscot. PhD thesis, Harvard

University.

Russell, Kevin. 1999. The "Word" in Two Polysynthetic Languages. *Studies on the Phonological Word*, ed. by T. Alan Hall and Ursula Kleinhenz, pp. 203–222. Amsterdam: John Benjamins.

Russell, Kevin, and Charlotte Reinholtz. 1997. Nonconfigurationality and the Syntax–Phonology Interface. *Proceedings of WCCFL 15*, ed. by Brian Agbayani and Sze-Wing Tang, pp. 441–456. Stanford, CA: CSLI Publications.

Salzmann, Zdenek, Andrew Cowell and Alonzo Moss, Sr. 2012. *Dictionary of the Arapaho Language*. 4th edn. Ethete, WY: Northern Arapaho Tribe.

Selkirk, Elisabeth O. 1984. *Phonology and Syntax: The Relation between Sound and Structure*. Cambridge, MA: MIT Press.

Selkirk, Elisabeth O. 1986. On Derived Domains in Sentence Phonology. *Phonology Yearbook* 3:371–405.

Selkirk, Elisabeth O. 1996. The Prosodic Structure of Function Words. *Signal to Syntax: Bootstrapping from Speech to Grammar in Early Acquisition*, ed. by James L. Morgan and Katherine Demuth, pp. 187–213. Mahwah, NJ: Lawrence Erlbaum Associates.

Selkirk, Elisabeth O. 2011. The Syntax–Phonology Interface. *The Handbook of Phonological Theory*, 2nd edn, ed. by John Goldsmith, Jason Riggle, and Alan C.L. Yu, pp. 435–484. Malden, MA: Wiley-Blackwell.

Slavin, Tanya. 2012. Phonological and Syntactic Evidence for Stem Structure in Oji-Cree. *International Journal of American Linguistics* 78:497–532.

Tallman, Adam J. R. 2021. Constituency and Coincidence in Chácobo (Pano). *Studies in Language* 45(2): 321–383.

Truitner, Kenneth L., and Timothy Dunnigan. 1975. Palatalization in Ojibwa. *Linguistic Inquiry* 6(2):301–316.

Weber, Natalie. 2020. Syntax, Prosody, and Metrical Structure in Blackfoot. PhD thesis, University of British Columbia.

Weber, Natalie. 2022. Prosodic Word Recursion in a Polysynthetic Language (Blackfoot; Algonquian). *Languages* 7(3):159. https://doi.org/10.3390/languages7030159.

Weber, Natalie, Tyler Brown, Joshua Celli, McKenzie Denham, Hailey Dykstra, Nico Kidd, Rodrigo Hernandez-Merlin, Evan Hochstein, Pinyu Hwang, Diana Kulmizev, Hannah Morrison, Matty Norris, and Lena Venkatraman. 2023. Blackfoot Words: A Database of Blackfoot Lexical Forms. *Language Resources and Evaluation*. https://doi.org/10.1007/s10579-022-09631-2.

Wolvengrey, Arok. 2001. *nêhiyawêwin: itwêwina / Cree: Words*. Regina: Canadian Plains Research Center.

Contributors

Antti Arppe is professor of quantitative linguistics at the University of Alberta, as well as the founder of the Alberta Language Technology Lab and the partnership director of the Social Sciences and Humanities Research Council funded partnership "21st Century Tools for Indigenous Languages." His research focuses on the documentation and computational modeling of Indigenous languages in North America, and the subsequent creation of digital resources and software tools for these languages, in order to support their revitalization efforts.

Ksenia Bogomolets (PhD, University of Connecticut 2020) serves as a principal language planning advisor at the Māori Language Commission, where she conducts research and provides guidance on the revitalization and maintenance of te reo Māori, New Zealand's indigenous language. Simultaneously, she continues her theoretical research as an honorary research fellow at the University of Auckland, primarily focusing on phonological and morphological influences on stress assignment across world languages.

Andrew Cowell (PhD, UC Berkeley 1993) is a professor of linguistics and faculty director of the Center for Native American and Indigenous Studies. He works in the areas of linguistic anthropology and language documentation. He has worked primarily on Arapaho, Gros Ventre, and Miwok, and has an interest in Polynesia (Hawaii and Tahiti in particular). He has published numerous articles and books, as well as developing curricular material and websites for language and culture learning and documentation. His current project is to develop a lexical database of Arapaho, with funding from the National Science Foundation / National Endowment for the Humanities Documenting Endangered Languages program.

Daniel Dacanay (/'dækənaɪ/, rhymes with 'smack a guy') is a computational linguist specializing in language documentation and revitalization who currently serves as the head linguist and dictionary keeper for the Tłı̨chǫ Government in Behchokǫ̀, Northwest Territories. In this role, he creates, expands, and maintains various Tłı̨chǫ language resources, notably the Tłı̨chǫ Online Dictionary. Dacanay completed his MSc in linguistics at the University of Alberta under Antti Arppe, with whom he also authored his honors thesis in 2022, and was a researcher at the Alberta Language Technology Lab. His research interests center on developing computational tools and resources for endangered languages, particularly in lexicography, morphosyntax, and semantics, with a primary focus on Plains Cree (nêhiyawêwin) and Dogrib (Tłı̨chǫ Yatıì). Additionally, he has contributed to online resources for Woods Cree (nīhithawīwin), Comox (ʔayʔaǰuθəm), and Sango, and assisted with dictionary creation for Sarcee (Tsúùt'ínà), Northern Haida (X̱aat Kíl), and Arapaho (Hinóno'éitíit), driven by his passion for preserving and empowering endangered languages worldwide.

Amy Dahlstrom is a professor emerita at the University of Chicago who investigates issues of morphology, syntax, semantics, and information structure in Algonquian languages, especially Meskwaki (Fox), spoken in Iowa, and Plains Cree, spoken in Saskatchewan and Alberta; her syntactic work is in the theoretical framework of Lexical Functional Grammar. Her research combines data from field elicitation with analysis of narrative texts, because textual attestations are particularly important for teasing out information structure relations such as topic and focus in languages with extremely flexible word order, and for understanding the role played by the discourse-based opposition within third person in Algonquian languages known as obviation. As part of her work with narrative texts, she has edited and translated portions of a remarkable corpus of texts (more than 27,000 pages) written in the Meskwaki syllabary by monolingual speakers in the early 20th century, making them available both to scholars and to members of the community who no longer read the traditional syllabary.

Rose-Marie Déchaine is a professor and chair of the African studies minor at the University of British Columbia, with research concentrations in syntactic theory, categorization, syntactic interface relations, and speech-gesture coordination. Her academic expertise spans field linguistics, syntax, and various interface areas including syntax-morphology, syntax-phonology, and syntax-semantics. Déchaine earned her PhD from the University of Massachusetts, Amherst (1993), MA from Université du Québec à Montréal (1986), and BA from the University of Alberta (1984). Her notable publications include works on binding domains, serial verb constructions, evidential types in Cree dialects, and the decomposition of pronouns.

Inge Genee is professor of linguistics at Iniskim University of Lethbridge. She teaches linguistics and Blackfoot grammar courses. She is the director of the Blackfoot Language Resources Lab and coeditor of the Blackfoot Digital Dictionary, both of which can be found at https://blackfoot.algonquianlanguages.ca/. She is also a coeditor of *Papers of the Algonquian Conference*. Her research is focused on Blackfoot grammar and the development of Blackfoot language revitalization resources and programming.

Erik D. Gooding is a professor of anthropology at Minnesota State University Moorhead. His research focuses on the Meskwaki and Thaaki.

Lily Lee Gooding is a student at the University of Oklahoma, in the Master of Legal Studies in Indigenous Peoples Law program. She received her undergraduate degree in criminal justice with an anthropology minor at Minnesota State University Moorhead. Her research focuses on Central Algonquian justice systems, past and present.

Stéphane Goyette est linguiste et professeur adjoint à l'Université Acadia en Nouvelle-Écosse (Canada). Il s'intéresse au contact langagier, notamment entre langues européennes et amérindiennes (surtout à l'époque coloniale).

Christopher Hammerly is an assistant professor in the Department of Linguistics at the University of British Columbia and director of the Experimental Linguistics and Fieldwork Lab. A descendant of the White Earth Nation in Minnesota, he focuses much of his research on understanding and documenting his ancestral language

Anishinaabemowin (Ojibwe). Hammerly employs diverse methodologies including formal theories, fieldwork, computational models, and experimental tasks to investigate cognitive representations and processes underlying human knowledge of syntax and morphology. His primary research interests center on the basic units of morphosyntax (person, number, and noun classification), their participation in long-distance dependencies such as movement and agreement, and the application of linguistics to develop curricula and technologies for language revitalization.

Dominik Kadlec received his BA in linguistics from the University of Calgary and his MA in Indigenous studies from the University of Lethbridge. His master's research was focused on creating a computational model of Blackfoot morphology that could be further developed and implemented for revitalization and documentation efforts. Currently, Dominik teaches classical languages to middle- and high school–aged students at the Alberta Classical Academy and continues to advocate for the preservation of endangered languages.

Robert E. Lewis Jr. is an enrolled member of the Citizen Potawatomi Nation. He obtained his PhD in linguistics from the University of Chicago. He is a curriculum and instruction manager for Prairie Band Potawatomi Nation's Language Department.

Cherry Meyer (she/her/hers) is an assistant professor with a joint appointment in the Departments of American Culture and Linguistics at the University of Michigan. A member of the Sault Ste. Marie Tribe of Chippewa Indians, she serves as core faculty in the Program in Native American Studies. Meyer's research focuses on Ojibwe (Algonquian), morphology, semantics, noun categorization, gender, classifiers, language documentation, language typology, and word order. She earned her PhD from the University of Chicago in 2020 and her BA from Wayne State University in 2012.

Sarah E. Murray is an associate professor of linguistics at Cornell University, as well as a graduate field member in American Indian and Indigenous Studies Program, Cognitive Science Program, and Department of Philosophy. Since 2006, she has been working with Chief Dull Knife College and the Cheyenne community in Montana on a variety of language projects.

Katherine Schmirler is currently conducting postdoctoral research at the University of Lethbridge, focusing on the computational modeling of Blackfoot. She recently completed her PhD in linguistics at the University of Alberta, where she worked on the 21st Century Tools for Indigenous Languages project with the Alberta Language Technology Lab (ALTLab). Her dissertation centered on creating a morphosyntactically tagged corpus for Plains Cree using an FST-based morphological model and Constraint Grammar parser.

Reed Steiner is a PhD student at the University of British Columbia whose research primarily focuses on the syntax-semantics interface through fieldwork on nɬeʔkepmxcín (a.k.a. "Thompson River Salish", ISO 639-3 language code: thp). His academic interests span field linguistics, formal-theoretical linguistics, morphology, Salish languages, semantics, syntax, and the syntax-semantics interface.

Rachel Vogel received her PhD in linguistics from Cornell University, where she studied the phonology of vowel devoicing both in Cheyenne and cross-linguistically. She has also researched methods of endangered language documentation and revitalization. She is currently pursuing a JD at Yale Law School.

Natalie Weber is an assistant professor in the Department of Linguistics at Yale University. Their main interests lie in phonology and the interfaces between phonology and other components of grammar. Since 2011, their empirical focus has been Blackfoot, an Algonquian language spoken in Alberta and northern Montana.

Anna Whitney is a PhD student in linguistics at the University of Michigan. Her work focuses on language contact and sociophonetics.